Mrs. Hannah Cowley

Which is the Man?

A Comedy

Mrs. Hannah Cowley

Which is the Man?
A Comedy

ISBN/EAN: 9783744661607

Printed in Europe, USA, Canada, Australia, Japan

Cover: Foto ©Thomas Meinert / pixelio.de

More available books at **www.hansebooks.com**

WHICH IS THE MAN?

A

COMEDY,

AS ACTED AT THE

THEATRE - ROYAL

IN

COVENT-GARDEN.

By Mrs. COWLEY.

THE FIFTH EDITION.

LONDON:

Printed for C. DILLY, in the Poultry.

1785.

It having been reported, that the Comedy was written by a

Military Character; a Gentleman of acknowledged genius

favoured the Author with the following

PROLOGUE,

Spoken by Mr. Lee Lewes, *dressed as an Officer.*

CALL'D forth Thalia's standard to display,
    And here maintain her sov'reign comic sway,
As Chief——I'll reconnoitre well the ground,
To learn what hostile lines are drawn around !
                    [*Surveys the House with a glass.*
    That's not a dark defile in yonder glade ; ——
For should it prove a treach'rous ambuscade,
No *puffing* miners have I here in pay,
To sap their works, or turn their covert way ;
No mercenary band who have been wont
To hack and hew like pioneers, in front !
    With flying shells our Engineers shall try
That well-mann'd battlement which tow'rs so high !
                    [*Pointing to the Upper Gallery.*
    Beneath, our point-blank shot will surely reach,
And in yon half-moon'd battery make a breach.
                    [*To the Second Gallery.*
    These lovely breast-works that adorn the field,
To Nature's gentle summons soon must yield !
                    [*Side-Boxes, &c.*
    This advanc'd post the picket-guard to keep,
And that reserve, who are entrench'd chin deep,
We hope to carry by a bold exertion,
At least amuse with some well-plann'd diversion !
                    [*To the Pit.*
    My troops are vet'rans :—it has been their lot,
To form in front of service hissing-hot ;
Who, when their ranks are gall'd, or put to flight,
Are sure to rally, and renew the fight,
Unless—and then no light-dragoons scour fleeter,
Their powder fails for want of true salt-petre !
    Our plan's avow'd ; it is from this firm station,
To gain the heights of public approbation !

DRAMATIS PERSONÆ.

M E N.

Lord Sparkle,	- - -	Mr. *Lee Lewes.*
Fitzherbert,	- - -	Mr. *Henderson.*
Beauchamp,	- - -	Mr. *Lewis.*
Belville,	- - -	Mr. *Wroughton.*
Pendragon,	- - -	Mr. *Quick.*

W O M E N.

Lady Bell Bloomer,	- -	Miss *Younge.*
Julia,	- - - - -	Miss *Satchell.*
Sophy Pendragon,	-	Mrs. *Mattocks.*
Clarinda,	- - - -	Mrs. *Morton.*
Kitty,	- - - -	Mrs. *Wilson.*
Tiffany,	- - - -	Mrs. *Davenett.*
Mrs. Johnson,	- - -	Miss *Platt.*

Ladies,	- -	Miss *Stewart,* Mrs. *Pouffin,* &c.
Gentlemen,	-	Mr. *Booth,* Mr. *Robson,* &c.

Servants to Lord Sparkle, Belville, Lady Bell, &c.

WHICH IS THE MAN?

ACT I. SCENE I.

A DRAWING-ROOM.   *Knock LH Door*

RH

.ter (*Mrs.* JOHNSON ~~croffes the Stage, a Boy following.~~)

Mrs. Johnf. HERE, Betty, Dick! Where are ye?
Don't you fee my Lord *Sparkle*'s car-
riage?—I fhall have my lodgers difturbed with their thun-
dering.——What, in the name of wonder, can bring him
here at this time in the morning?——Here he comes, looking like a rake as he is!

LH Enter LORD SPARKLE (*yawning*).

Spark. Bid 'em turn; I fha'nt ftay a moment.——So,
Mrs. *Johnfon,* I pull'd the ftring juft to fee how your Syl-
vans go on.

Mrs. Johnf. As ufual, my Lord; but, blefs me! how
early your Lordfhip is!

Spark. How late, you mean.—I have not been in bed
fince yefterday at one!—I am going home now to reft for
an hour or two, and then to the Drawing-room.—But what
are the two ruftics about? I have not been plagued with
them thefe three or four days.

Mrs. Johnf. They are now out.

Spark. I fuppos'd that, or I fhould not have call'd.——
But prithee, do they talk of returning to their native woods
again?

B   *Mrs.*

Mrs. Johns. Oh no, Sir!—The young gentleman feems to have very different ideas:—Mifs, too, has great fpirits, though fhe feems now and then at a lofs what to do with herfelf.

Spark. Do with herfelf! Why don't you perfuade her to go back to Cornwall? You fhould tell 'em what a vile place London is, full of fnares, and debaucheries, and witch-crafts.—You don't *preach* to 'em, *Johnfon.*

Mrs. Johnf. Inde d I do, my Lord; and their conftant anfwer is, "Oh, Lord *Sparkle* is our friend? Lord *Sparkle* "would take it amifs if we fhould go; 'twould look like "diftrufting his Lordfhip."

Spark. Was ever man fo hamper'd!—Two fools! to miftake common forms and civilities for attachments.

Mrs. Johnf. I fear, my Lord, towards the young Lady fomething *more* than forms——

Spark. (interrupting) Never, upon my honour!—I kiffed her; fo I did all the women in the parifh—the feptennial ceremony. The brother I us'd to drink vile Port with, liften to his village-ftories, call his vulgarity wit, and his impudence fpirit; was not that fatigue and mortification enough, but I muft be *bored* with 'em here in Town?

Mrs. Johnf. But, *Mifs*, Sir, talks of preffing invitations and letters, and——

Spark. Things of courfe; they had influence, and got me the borough. I, in return, faid fhe was the moft charm-ing girl in the world; that I ador'd her; and fome few things that every body fays on fuch occafions, and nobody thinks of.

Mrs. Johnf. But it appears that Mifs *did* think——

Spark. Yes, 'fa'th: and on my writing a civil note that I fhould be happy to fee them in Town, *et cætera*—which I meant to have fufpended our acquaintance till the General Election—they took me at my Word; and before I thought the letter had reach'd 'em, they were in my houfe, all joy and congratulation. I didn't chufe to be encumber'd with 'em, fo placed 'em with you. The Boy was at firft amu-fing, but our Circles have had him, and I muft be rid of him.

Mrs. Johnf. I muft fay, I wifh I was quit of them at prefent; for my conftant lodger Mr. *Belville* came to town laft night, and he wants this drawing-room to himfelf: he's oblig'd to fhare it now with Mr. *Pendragon* and his fifter.

Spark.

Spark. Hey! *Belville!*—'Gad, that's lucky! There is not a fellow in Town better receiv'd by the women.—Throw the girl in his way, and get quit of her at once.

Mrs. Johnf. If you mean diſhoneſtly, my Lord, you have miſtaken your perſon: I did not live ſo many years with your mother to be capable of ſuch a thing.—Ah, my Lord, if my Lady were living——

Spark. She would ſcold to little purpoſe,---and you may ſpare yourſelf the trouble.——I tell you, I care nothing about the girl: I merely want to get rid of her, and you muſt aſſiſt me.—*(Mrs. Johnſon turns from him with diſguſt)*——Hey-dey! the nicety of your Ladyſhip's honour is piqued! Ha! ha! ha!—the miſtreſs of a lodging-houſe!—*Bien drole*—Ha! ha! ha! ［*Exit Mrs.* Johnſon. *RH*

But who is this hobbling up ſtairs?—Ha! old Cato the Cenſor, my honourable couſin!—What the devil ſhall I do?—No avoiding him, however.—

LH Enter Mr. FITZHERBERT.

I wiſh I had been out of the houſe, *Fitzherbert,* before you appeared! I know I ſhall not eſcape without ſome abuſe.

Fitz. I never throw away reproof, where there are no hopes of amendment—your Lordſhip is ſafe.

Spark. Am I to take that for wit?

Fitz. No; for then I fear you would not underſtand it.

Spark. Poſitively, you muſt give me more of the felicity of your converſation: I want you to teach me ſome of that happy eaſe which you poſſeſs in your rudeneſs; 'twould be to me an acquiſition. I am eternally getting into the moſt horrid ſcrapes, merely by politeneſs and good-breeding.—Here are two perſons now in this houſe, for inſtance——

Fitz. (interrupting) Who do *not* know, that the language of what *you* call politeneſs, differs from that of truth and honour.—You ſee I know thoſe to whom you allude.—But we only loſe time!—Good day, my Lord!

Spark. Loſe time! Ha! ha! ha!—Why, of what value can time be to you? the greateſt enemy you have, adding every day to your wrinkles and ill-humour. I'll prove to you now, that I have employ'd the laſt twelve hours to better purpoſe than you have. Nine of them you ſlept away—the laſt three you have been running about Town, *ſnarling* and making people uneaſy with themſelves;—whilſt I

have

р /* harmless */

222222

have been fitting peaceably at Welijie's, where I have won—guefs what?

Fitz. Half as much as you loft yefterday—a thoufand or two guineas, perhaps.

Spark. Guineas! Poh! you are jefting! Guineas are as fcarce with us, as in the coffers of the Congrefs. Like them we ftake with counters, and play for folid earth.

Fitz. (impatiently) Well!

Spark. Bullion is a mercantile kind of wealth, paffing thro' the hands of dry-falters, vinegar-merchants, and Lord-Mayors!—Our Goddefs holds a cornucopia inftead of a purfe from which fhe pours corn-fields, fruitful vallies, and rich herds. This morning fhe popp'd into my dice-box a fnug villa, five hundred acres, arable and pafture, with the next prefentation to the living of Guzzleton.

Fitz. A church-living in a dice-box! Well, well; I fuppofe it will be beftow'd as worthily as it was gain'd!---Good day, my Lord, good day! *[Turning from him.* X

Spark. Good night, Crabtree—good night! *[Going off.*

RH *Enter a* SERVANT.

Tell *Belville* I call'd to congratulate his efcape from the ftupid country. *[Going.*

Fitz. My Lord!

Spark. (returning) Sir!

Fitz. I am going this morning to vifit Lady *Bell Bloomer.*—I give you this intimation, that we may not rifk another rencontre.

Spark. Civilly defign'd; and for the fame polite reafon I inform you, that I fhall be there in the evening.

[Exit Lord Sparkle.

Fitz. Your mafter in bed yet! What time was he in Town yefterday?

Serv. Late, Sir.—We fhould have been earlier, but we met with Sir Harry Hairbrain on the road, with his new fox-hounds.—Fell in with the hunt at Bagfhot—broke cover, run the firft burft acrofs the heath towards Datchet;---fhe then took right an end for Egham, funk the wind upon us as far as Staines, where Reynard took the road to Oxford, and we the route to Town, Sir. *[Bowing.*

Fitz. Very geographical indeed, Sir.---Now, pray inform your mafter——Oh, here we come!

Enter

RH Enter BELVILLE *in a robe de chambre.*

Juft rifen from your pillows!——Are you not afham'd of this? A fox-hunter, and in bed at eleven!

Belv. My dear, morofe, charming, quarrelfome old friend, I am ever in character!—In the country, I defy fatigue and hardfhip.—Up before the lazy flut Aurora has put on her pink-coloured gown to captivate the plough-boys—fcamper over hedge and ditch. Dead with hunger, alight at a cottage; drink milk from the hands of a brown wench, and eat from a wooden platter. In Town, I am a fine gentleman; have my hair exactly dreffed; my cloaths *au dernier gout*; dine on made-difhes; drink Burgundy; and, in a word, am every-where the *ton*.

Fitz. So much the worfe, fo much the worfe, young man! To be the *ton* where Vice and Folly are the ruling deities, proves that you muft be fometimes a fool, at others a——

Belv. (interrupting) Pfha! you fatirifts, like moles, fhut your eyes to the light, and grope about for the dark fide of the human character: there is a great deal of good-fenfe and good-meaning in the world. As for its follies, I think folly a mighty pleafant thing; at leaft, to play the fool *gracefully*, requires more talents than would fet up a dozen cynics.

Fitz. Then half the people I know muft have *wonderful* talents, for they have been playing the fool from fixteen to fixty.——*Apropos!* I found my precious kinfman Lord *Sparkle* here.

Belv. Ay! there's an inftance of the happy effects of total indifference to the fage maxims you recommend.

Fitz. Happy effects do you call them?

Belv. Moft triumphant! Who fo much admired? who fo much the fafhion?—the general favourite of the Ladies, and the common object of imitation with the men. Is not Lord *Sparkle* the happy man, who's to carry the rich and charming widow Lady *Bell Bloomer* from fo many rivals? —And will not you, after quarreling with him half your life, leave him a fine eftate at the end of it?

Fitz. No, no!—I tell you, No! [*With warmth.*

Belv. Nay, his fuccefs with the widow is certain.—He boafts his triumph every-where; and as fhe is fuch a favourite of yours, every thing elfe will follow.

Fitz. No; for if fhe marries *Sparkle*, fhe will be no longer a favourite. Yet fhe receives him with a degree of diftinction

diftinction that fometimes makes me fear it; for we frequently fee women of accomplifhments and beauty, to which every heart yields homage, throw themfelves into the arms of the debauched, the filly, and the vain.

LH Enter a SERVANT.

Serv. Mr. *Beauchamp.* [*Exit. L*

Fitzb. Oh! I expected him to call on you this morning. You muft obtain his confidence; it will affift me in my defigns. When I found myfelf difappointed in my hopes of his Lordfhip, I felected *Beauchamp* from the younger branches of my family: but of this he knows nothing, and thinks himfelf under high obligations to the patronage of the Peer; an error in which I wifh him to continue, as it will give me an opportunity of proving them both.——But here he comes!—This way I can avoid him. [*Exit. R*

LH Enter BEAUCHAMP.

Belv. *Beauchamp!*——and in regimentals!——Why, prithee, *George,* what fpirit has feized thee now? When I faw thee laft, thou wert devoted to the grave profeffion of the Law, or the Church; and I expected to have feen thee invelop'd in wig, wrangling at the bar; or feated in a fat benefice, receiving tythe-pigs and poultry.

Beauch. Thofe, *Belville,* were my fchool-defigns; but the fire of youth gave me ardors of a different fort. The heroes of the Areopagus and the Forum have yielded to thofe of Marathon; and I feel, that whilft my country is ftruggling amidft furrounding foes, I ought not to devote a life to learned indolence, that might be glorioufly hazarded in her defence.

Belv. (*fmiling*) I fhan't give you credit now for that fine flourifh.——This fudden ardor for " the pride, pomp, and circumftance of glorious war,"—I dare fwear this heroic fpirit fprings from the whim of fome fine Lady, who fancied you would be a fmarter fellow in a cockade and gorget, than in a ftiff band and perriwig.

Beauch. If your infinuation means that my heart has not been infenfible of the charms of fome fair Lady, you are right; but my transformation is owing to no whim of her's: for, oh *Charles!* fhe never yet condefcended to make me the object of her thoughts.

Belv. Modeft too!—Ay, you were right to give up the Law,

Law. – But who, pray, may this exalted Fair-one be who never *condefcended* ?

Beauch. I never fuffer my lips to wanton with the charming founds that form her name. I have a kind of milady felicity in glating on her dear idea, that would be impaired, fhould it be known to exift in my heart.

Belv. Ha! ha! ha! who *can* be the nymph who has infpired fo *obfolete* a paffion? —In the days of chivalry it wou'd have been the *un.*

Beauch. I will gratify you thus far: The Lady has beauty, wit, and fpirit; but, above all, a *mind.*—Is it poffible, *Charles,* to love a woman without a mind ?

Belv. Has fhe a mind for you? That is the moft important queftion.

Beauch. I dare not feed my paffion with fo prefumptuous a hope; yet I would not extinguifh it, if I could: for it is not a love that tempts me into corners to wear out my days in complaints: it prompts me to ufe them for the moft important purpofes:—the ardors it gives me, fhall be felt in the land of our enemies; they fhall know how *well* I love.

Belv. Poh! poh! this is the gallantry of One Thoufand One Hundred and One; the kind of paffion that animated our fathers in the fields of Creffy and Poictiers.——Why, no Beauty of our age, man, will be won in this ftile!—— Now, fuppofe yourfelf at the Opera *(looking through his hand)* " Gad, that's a fine girl! Twenty thoufand, you " fay? I think I'll have her. Yes, fhe'll do! I—I muft " have her! I'll call on her to-morrow and tell her fo." Have you fpirit and courage enough for that, my Achilles ?

Beauch. No truly.

Belv. Then give up all thoughts of being received.

Beauch. I have no thoughts of hazarding a reception. The pride of birth, and a few hundreds for my education, were the fole patrimony the imprudence of a father left me. My relation Lord *Sparkle* has procured for me a commiffion. —Generoufly to offer that and a knapfack to a Lady of five thoufand a-year, would be properly anfwered by a contemptuous difmiffion.

Belv. But fuppofe fhe fhould take a fancy to your knapfack ?

Beauch. That would reduce *me* to the neceffity of depriving *myfelf* of a happinefs I would die to obtain; for

never

never can I submit to be quartered on a Wife's fortune, whilst I have a sword to carve subsistence for myself.

Belv. That may be in the *great* stile; but 'tis scarcely in the *polite.* Will you take chocolate in my dressing-room?

Beauch. No; I am going to take orders at my Colonel's: where shall we meet in the evening?

Belv. 'Faith, 'tis impossible to tell! I commit myself to Chance for the remainder of the day, and shall finish it as she directs.   [*Exeunt at opposite sides.*

2^d Scene changes to an Apartment at CLARINDA'S.

Enter CLARINDA, *reading a Catalogue, followed by* TIFFANY.

Clar. Poor Lady Squander! So Christie has her jewels and furniture at last!——I must go to the sale.——Mark that Dresden service, and the pearls. *(Gives the catalogue to the Maid)* It must be a great comfort to her to see her jewels worn by her friends.—Who was here last night? *(sitting down, and taking some cards from the table)* I came home so late, I forgot to enquire!——Mrs. *Jessamy*—Lady *Racket*—Miss *Belvoir*—Lord *Sparkle* *(starting up)*—Lord *Sparkle* here! Oh Heavens and earth! what possessed me to go to Lady *Price's?* I wish she and her concert of three fiddles and a flute had been playing to her kids on the Welsh mountains!—Why did you persuade me to go out last night?

Tiff. Dear ma'am, you seem'd so low-spirited, that I thought——

Clar. I missed him every-where!—At four places he was just gone as I came in.—But what does it signify?—'Twas Lady *Bell Bloomer* he was seeking, I dare swear; his attachment to the *relict* is every-where the subject. Hang those widows! I really believe there's something ca-balistical in their names.—No less than fourteen fine young fellows of fortune have been drawn into the matrimonial noose by them since last February.——'Tis well they were threatened with imprisonment, or we should not have had an unmarried Infant above seventeen, between Charing-Cross and Portman-Square.

Tiff. Well, I am sure I wish Lady *Bell* was married; she's always putting you out of temper.

Clar. Have I not cause? Till she broke upon the Town, I was at the top of fashion—you know I was. My dress, my equipage, my furniture, and myself, were the criterions of tafte; but a new French chamber-maid enabled her Ladyfhip at one ftroke to turn the tide againft me..

Tiff. Ay, I don't know what good thefe Mademoifelles——

Clar. (interrupting) But, *Tiffany,* fhe is to be at court to-day, out of mourning for the firft time : I am refolved to be there.——No, I won't go ~~neither, now I think on't.~~——If fhe fhou'd really outfhine me, her triumph will be increafed by my being witnefs to it.——I won't go to St. James's; but I'll go to her route this evening, and, if 'tis poffible, prevent Lord *Sparkle*'s being particular to her.—— Perhaps that will put her in an ill-humour, and then the advantage will be on my fide.   [*Exit* Clarinda. *LH*

Tiff. Mercy on us! To be a chamber-maid to a *Mifs* on the brink of Thirty requires as good politics, as being Prime Minifter! Now, if fhe fhould not rife from her toilette quite in looks to-day, or if the defertion of a lover, or the victory of a rival, fhould happen, ten to one but I fhall be forced to refign without even a Penfion to retire on.   [*Exit* Tiffany. *LH*

END OF THE FIRST ACT.

21, Minifter.

C   ACT

ACT II. SCENE I.

An elegant Apartment at LADY BELL BLOOMER's.

Enter JULIA, *with Papers in her Hand.*

Julia. WHAT an invaluable treasure! Those dear papers, that have lain within the frigid walls of a Convent, insensible, and uninteresting to every one around them, contain for *me* a world of happiness. He is in England! How little he suspects that *I* too am here!

Enter KITTY.

Kitty. Mr. *Fitzherbert* will be here immediately, Ma'am.

Julia. Mr. *Fitzherbert!* Very well. Has Lady *Bell* finished dressing yet?

Kitty. (speaking exceedingly fast) No, Ma'am.—Mr. *Crape* the hair-dresser has been with her these three hours, and her maid is running here and there, and Mr. *John* flying about to milliners and perfumers, and the new *vis-a-vis* at the door to carry her Ladyship to court.—Every thing black banished, and the liveries come home shining with silver; and the moment she's gone out, every body will be in such a delightful hurry about the route that her Ladyship is to give this evening; that they say all the world——

Julia. Ha! ha! ha! Prithee stop! I can't wonder if Lady *Bell* shou'd be transported at dropping her weeds, for it seems to have turn'd the heads of the whole family.

Kitty. Oh! dearee, Ma'am, to be sure! for now we shall be so gay! Lady *Bell* has such fine spirits!——And 'tis well she has; for the servants tell me, their old master would have broke her heart else.—They all adore her!—— I wish you were a little gayer, Ma'am!——Somehow we are so dull!—'Tis a wonder so young and so pretty a Lady—

Julia. Don't run into impertinence.—I have neither the taste nor talents for public life that Lady *Bell Bloomer* has.

Kitty. Laws, Ma'am, 'tis all use! *You* are always at home; but Lady *Bell* knows, that wit and a fine person are not given for a fire-side *at home (drawling)*. She shines every

Table
&Chairs.

_T._

Papers & Bouquet on Do. Vase

Ly Bell. (without R.) Walk the Carriage
— round immediately —

evening in half the houfes of half-a-dozen parifhes, and
the next morning we have ftanzas in the *Bevy of Beauties*,
and fonnets, and billets-doux, and all the fine things that
fine Ladies are fo fond of.

Julia. ~~I can bear your freedoms no longer!~~ *Here*—Carry thefe
flowers with my compliments, and tell her Ladyfhip I fent
to Richmond for them, as I know her fondnefs for natural
bouquets ; and bid Harry deny me to every body this morning, except Mr. *Fitzherbert*.

[*Exit* Kitty. *RH*

LH Enter Mr. FITZHERBERT.

Fitz. Happily excepted, my dear Ward ! But I fuppofe
you heard my ftep, and threw in my name for a douceur.
I can hardly believe, that when you fhut your doors on
youth and flattery, you would open them to a crofs old
man, who feldom entertains you with any thing but your
faults.

Julia. How you miftake, Sir ! You are the greateft
flatterer I have: your whole conduct flatters me with efteem,
and love ; and as you do not *fquander* thefe things——
(*fmiling*)

Fitz. There I muft correct you.——I do fquander them
on few objects, indeed; and they are proportionably
warmer. I feel attachments fifty times as ftrong as your
good-humour'd fmiling people, who are every one's humble fervant, and every body's friend. Where is Lady
Bell ?

Julia. Yet at her toilette, I believe. My dear Sir, I am
every hour more grateful to you, for having given me fo
charming a friend.

Fitz. So I would have you. When you came from
France, I prevailed on her Ladyfhip to allow you her
fociety, that you might add to the polifh of elegant manners the graces of an elegant mind. Here fhe comes ! her
tongue and her heels keeping time.

Lady Bell. Oh you monfter! But I am in fuch divine spirits, that nothing you fay can deftroy them.——My fweet *Julia,* what a bouquet! Lady Myrtle will expire.——She was fo envelop'd in flowers and ever-greens laft night, that fhe look'd like the picture of fair Rofamond in her bower. ——My dear *Fitz,* do you know we dined yefterday in Hill-ftreet, and had the fortitude to ftay till eleven!

Julia. I was tired to death with the fatiguing vifit.

Lady Bell. Now I, on the contrary, came away with frefh relifh for fociety. The perfevering civility of Sir Andrew and the maukifh infipidity of his tall daughter act like olives: You can't endure them on your palate, but they heghten the gufto of your Tokay.

Fitz. Then I advife your Ladyfhip to ferve up Sir Andrew and his daughter at your next entertainment.

Lady Bell. So I would, only one can't remove 'em with the deffert. But how do you like me? ~~Did you ever fee fo delightful a head?~~ Don't you think I fhall make a thoufand conquefts to-day?

Fitz. Doubtlefs, if you meet with fo many fools.——But pray, which of thofe you have already made, will be the moft flattered by all thefe gay infignia of your liberty?

Lady Bell. Probably, he whom it leaft concerns.

Julia. Pray tell us which is that?

Lady Bell. Oh, Heavens! to anfwer that, requires more reflection than I have ever given the fubject.

Julia. Should you build a temple to your lovers, I fancy we fhould find Lord *Sparkle's* name on the altar.

Lady Bell. Oh! Lord *Sparkle!*——Who can refift the gay, the elegant, the all-conquering Lord *Sparkle?* the moft diftinguifhed feather in the plume of fafhion——~~without that barbarous ftrength of mind which gives impor- tance to virtues or to views~~ Fafhionable, becaufe he's well dreft:——Brilliant, becaufe he's of the firft Clubs, and ufes his borrowed wit like his borrowed gold, as tho' it was his own.

Fitz. Why, now, this man, whom you underftand fo well, you receive as tho' his tinfel was pure gold.

Lady Bell. Aye, to be fure!——Tinfel is juft as well for fhew.——~~The world is charitable, and accepts tinfel for gold in moft cafes.~~

Fitz. But in the midft of all this funfhine for Lord *Sparkle,* will you not throw a ray on the fpirited, modeft *Beauchamp?*

Lady Bell.

2.

Lady Bell. A ray of favour for *Beauchamp!*—Were I so inclined, to make it welcome, I must change my fan for a spear, my feathers for a helmet, and stand forth a Thalestris. —You know *his* mistress is War—*(sighing, and then recovering).*—But why do I trifle thus?—The hour of triumph is at hand.

Fitz. Of what? hour

Lady Bell. The moment of triumph!—*Anglice*, the moment when, having shewn myself at half the houses in St. George's, I am set down at St. James's, my fellows standing on each hand, as I descend—the whisper flying through the croud, " Who is she? Who is that sweet creature?— " One of the four heiress's?"—" No; she's a foreign am- " bassadress."——I ascend the stairs—move slowly thro' the rooms—drop my fan—incommode my bouquet—stay to adjust it, that the *little* gentry may have time to fix their admiration—again move on—enter the Drawing-room— throw a flying glance round the Circle, and see nothing but spite in the eyes of the women, and a thousand nameless things in those of the men.

Julia. The very soul of giddiness!

Lady Bell. The very soul of happiness!—Can I be less? —Think of a widow just emerg'd from her weeds for a hus- band to whom her *father*, not her *heart*, united her—my jointure elegant—my figure charming—deny it if you dare! ——Pleasure, Fortune, Youth, Health, all opening their stores before me; whilst Innocence and conscious Honour shall be my handmaids, and guide me in safety through the dangerous ordeal.

Fitz. To your Innocence and conscious Honour add, if you have time *(archly)*, a little Prudence, or your centinels may be surpris'd asleep, and you reduc'd to a disgraceful capitulation.

Lady Bell. Oh! I'm mistress of my whole situation, and cannot be surpris'd.——But, Heav'ns! I am losing a con- quest every moment I stay!—The Loves and Pleasures have prepared their rosy garlands—my triumphal car is waiting —and my proud steeds neighing to be gone.——Away to victory!——   [*Exit with great spirit.*

Fitz. A charming woman, *Julia!*—She conceals a fine understanding under apparent giddiness; and a most sensible heart beneath an air of indifference.

Julia. Yes, I believe her Ladyship's heart is more sensible than she allows to herself. I rally her on Lord *Sparkle*, but
                                          it

it is Mr. *Beauchamp*, whose name is never mentioned but her cheeks tell such blushing truths, as she wou'd never forgive me for observing.

Fitz. Upon my word, you seem well acquainted with your friend's heart!——Will you be equally frank as to your own?

Julia. (in great confusion) Sir!——my heart!

Fitz. Yes; will you assist me in reading it?

Julia. To be sure, Sir.

Fitz. Then tell me, if amongst the ~~painted, powdered,~~ gilded moths whom your beauty or fortune have allured, is there *one* whom you would honour with your hand?—— Aye, take time; I would not have you precipitate.

Julia. (hesitatingly) No, Sir—not one.

Fitz. I depend on your truth, and on that assurance inform you, that a friend of mine is arriv'd in town, whom I mean this morning to present to you.

Julia. As a——

Fitz. As a lover, who has my warmest wishes that he may become your husband.

Julia. Do I know the person for whom you are thus interested, Sir?

Fitz. You do not; but I have had long intimacy with him, and 'tis the dearest wish of my heart to see him and *Julia Manners* united.

Julia. I trust, Sir, you will allow——

Fitz. Be under no apprehensions.——Much as I'm interested in this union, your inclinations shall be attended to. —I am now going to your lover, and shall introduce him to you this morning.——Come, don't look so distress'd, child, at the approach of that period which will give you *dignity* and *character* in society.—The marriage-state is that in which your sex evinces its importance; and where, in the interesting circle of domestic duties, a woman has room to exercise every virtue that constitutes the Great and the Amiable.   *LH* [*Exit* Fitzherbert.

Julia. The moment I so much dreaded is arrived! How shall I reveal to my Guardian, and to Lady *Bell*, that I *am* married? that I have already dared to take on me those important duties? I must not reveal it—my solemn promise to my husband—But where is he?—Oh! I must write to him this moment, that I may not be left defenceless to brave the storm of offended authority, and love. *RH* [*Exit* Julia.

$$\overline{3.} \quad \underline{\text{Polarès}.}$$

$\nwarrow$ Pere. Speaks without R.

SCENE II. BELVILLE's *Lodgings.* 2*G*

RH Enter BELVILLE *new-dreſt.*

Belv. Let my trunks be ready, and the chaiſe at the door to-morrow morning by ſix, for I ſhall dine in Dover.

Ii Fitz. Ha! juſt in time, I ſee!—You are ready plumed for flight.

Belv. True; but my flight wou'd have been to you.— Impatient to know the cauſe of your ſummoning me from the Dryades and Hamadryades of Berkſhire, your letter reach'd me at the very inſtant I was ſetting out for Dover, in my way to Paris.

Fitz. Paris!

Belv. Yes.

Fitz. Poh! poh! ſtay where you are, ſtay where you are! The great turnpike between Dover and Calais is a road de-ſtructive to this kingdom; and I wiſh there were toll-gates erected on its confines, to reſtrain with a *heavy tax* the number of its travellers.

Belv. I fear the *tax* would be more generally felt than the *benefit*; for it would reſtrain not only the folly-mongers and the faſhion-mongers, but the rational enquirer and the travelling connoiſſeur.

Fitz. So much the better! ſo much the better!—Our travelling philoſophers have done more towards deſtroying the nerves of their country, than all the politics of France. Their chief aim ſeems to be, to eſtabliſh infidelity, and to captivate us with deluſive views of manners ſtill more im-moral and licentious than our own.—Hey-dey! who's this?—Oh, the Corniſh lad, I ſuppoſe, whom Lord *Sparkle* placed here.

Belv. (laughing) Yes; an odd being!—He was deſigned by nature for a Clodpole; but the notice of a Peer overſet the little underſtanding he had, and ſo he commenced fine gentleman. He has a ſiſter with him, who ran wild upon the commons till her father's death; but ſhe fancies her-ſelf a wit, and ſatirizes Bruin.—Here he comes.

RH Enter PENDRAGON.

Pen. My dear fellow-lodger, I'm come to——Oh! your ſervant, Sir! (*to* Fitzherbert)—Is this gentleman a friend of yours?

Belv. He is.

Pen.

Pen. Your hand, Sir! (*passes* Belville, *and stands between them*)—If you are Mr. Belville's friend, you are my friend, and we are all friends; I soon make acquaintance.

Fitz. A great happiness!

Pen. Yes, so it is, and very polite too I have been in the Great World almost six weeks, and I can see no difference between the Great World and the Little World, only that they've no ceremony; and so as that's the mark of good-breeding, I tries to hit it off.

Fitz. With success.

Pen. To convince you of that, I'll tell you a devilish good thing.—You must know——

Fitz. (*interrupting*) Excuse me now, but I am convinc'd you will amuse me, and desire your company at dinner—they'll give you my address below. Mr. Belville, I have business of importance.

                         [*Exit* Fitzherbert *and* Belville.

Pen. Gad, I'm glad he ask'd me to visit him!—He must be a Lord by his want of ceremony. (*imitating*) " Mr. Belville, I have business of importance"—and off they go. —Now in Cornwall we should have thought that damn'd rude—but 'tis easy.—" Mr. Belville, I have business of importance."—(*going*) Easy—easy—easy!

         Enter SOPHY PENDRAGON.

Sophy. Brother Bobby!—Brother Bobby!

Pen. (*returning*) I desire, Miss Pendragon, you won't brother me at this rate—making one look as if one didn't know Life.—How often shall I tell you, that it is the most ungenteel thing in the world for relations to *Brother*, and *Father*, and *Cousin* one another, and all that sort of thing. I did not get the better of my shame for three days, when you bawl'd out to Mrs. Dobson at Launceston Concert— " Aunt, Aunt, here's room between Brother and I, if Cousin Dick will sit closer to Father!"

Sophy. Lack-a-day!—and where's the harm? What d'ye think one has relations given one for?—To be asham'd of 'em?

Pen. I don't know what they were given us for; but I know no young man of fashion *cares* for his relations.

Sophy. More shame for your young men of fashion; but I assure you, Brother Bobby, I shall never give in to any such unnatural, new-fangled ways. As for you, since Lord *Sparkle* took notice of you, you are quite another thing.

thing. You used to creep into the parlour, when Father
had company, hanging your head like a dead partridge;
steal all round the room behind their backs to get at a
chair; then fit down on one corner of it, tying knots in
your handkerchief; and if any-body drank your health,
rise up, and scrape your foot so—"Thank you kindly,
Sir!"—

Pen. By Goles, if you—(*shaking his fist*)

Sophy. But now, when you enter a room, your hat is
toss'd carelessly on a table; you pass the company with a
half bend of your body; fling yourself into one chair, and
throw your legs on another:—"Pray, my dear Sir, do
me the favour to ring."—"John, bring Lemonade."—
"Mrs. Plume has been driving me all morning in Hyde-
Park, against the wind, and the dust has made my throat
mere plaister of Paris."—

Pen. Hang me, if I don't like myself at second-hand
better than I thought I should!—Why, if I do it as well
as you, *Sophy,* I shall soon be quite the thing!—And
now I'll give you a bit of advice:—As 'tis very certain
Lord *Sparkle* means to introduce you to High Life, 'tis
fitting you should know how to behave; and as I have
been amongst 'em, I can tell you.

Sophy. Well!

Pen. Why, first of all, if you should come into a drawing-room, and find twenty or thirty people in the circle,
you are not to take the least notice of any one.

Sophy. No!

Pen. No! The servant will, perhaps, get you a
chair;—if not, slide into the nearest. The conversation
will not be interrupted by your entrance; for they'll take
as little notice of you, as you of them.

Sophy. Psha!

Pen. Then, be sure to be equally indifferent to the
coming-in of others.—I saw poor Lady Carmine one
night dying with confusion, for the vulgarity and ill-
breeding of her friend, who actually rose from her chair,
at the entrance of the Dutchess of Dulcet and Lady Betty
Blowze.

Sophy. Be quiet, *Bobby!*

Pen. True, as I am a young man of fashion!—Then
you must never let your discourse go beyond one word.—If
any body should happen to take the trouble to entertain
the company, you may throw in—"Charming!—Odious!
—Capital!"

D

—Capital!"—Never mount to a phrase, unless to that dear delightful one, of " all that sort of thing."—The use made of that is wonderful!—" *All that sort of thing*," is an apology for want of wit; it is a substitute for argument; it will serve for the point of a story, or the fate of a battle.

Sophy. Well then,—upon going away ?

Pen. Oh, you go away as you came in !—If one has a mind to give the lady of the house a nod, (*nodding*) one may; but 'tis still higher breeding to leave *her* with as little ceremony as *I* do you. [*Exit* Pendragon *without looking at her.*

Sophy. I wish I could be sure it was the fashion not to mind forms, I'd go directly and visit Lord *Sparkle*. I could tear my eyes out to think I was abroad to-day when he call'd on Mrs. *Johnson!*—In all the books I have read, I never met with a lover so careless as he is.—Sometimes I have a mind to treat him with disdain, and then I recollect all I have read about Ladies behaviour that break their Lovers hearts;—but he won't come near me.—Now I have been three days in a complying humour—but 'tis all one; still he keeps away. I'll be hang'd, if I don't know what he's about soon!—He shan't think to bring me from the Land's End to make a fool of me: *Sophy Pendragon* has more spirit than he thinks for.

[*Exit* Sophy.

Re-enter FITZHERBERT *and* BELVILLE.

Bel. A Wife! Heaven's last best gift!—But—a—no—I shan't marry yet. I have a hundred little follies to act before I do so rash a thing.

Fitz. But I say, you *shall* marry. I have studied you from eighteen, and know your character, your faults, and your virtues; and such as you are, I have pick'd you out from all the blockheads and fools about you, to take a fine girl off my hands with twenty thousand pounds.

Belv. 'Tis a bribe, doubtless!—But what *is* the Lady; Coquet, Prude, or Vixen ?

Fitz. You may make her what you will. Treat her with confidence, tenderness, and respect, and she'll be an angel; be morose, suspicious, and neglectful, and she'll be—a woman.—The Wife's character and conduct is a comment on that of the Husband.

R. A. B.

Belv. (*gaily*) Any thing more ?—

Fitz. Yes, she is my ward, and the daughter of the friend of my youth.—I entertain parental affection for her, and give you the highest proof of my esteem in transferring to *you* the care of her happiness. Refuse it, if you dare.

Belv. Dare! My dear friend, I *must* refuse the honour you offer me.

Fitz. How !

Belv. To be serious, it is not in my power to wed the Lady.

Fitz. I understand you.—I am disappointed !—I should have mentioned this subject to you, before I had suffered it to make so strong a feature in my picture of future happiness.

Bel. Would you had, that I might have informed you at once—that I am—married.

Fitz. Married !—Where, when, how, with whom ?

Belv. Where ?—In France.——*When ?*—About eight months since.——*How ?*—By an English clergyman.——*With whom ?*—Ah, with such a one !——Her beauty is of the Greek kind, which pleases the mind more than the eye.—Yet to the eye nothing can be more lovely.—To this charming creature add the name of *Julia Manners*, and you know my wife.

Fitz. Julia Manners ! Julia Manners did you say ?

Belv. Yes, *Julia Manners !* I first knew her at the house of a friend in Paris, whose daughters were in the same convent with herself. I often visited her at the grate; at length, by the assistance of Mademoiselle St. Val, prevailed on her to give me her hand, but was immediately torn from her by a summons from my uncle at Florence; whence I was dispatched to England on a ministerial affair.

Fitz. So, so, so, very fine ! (*aside*)——I suppose you had the prudence to make yourself acquainted with the Lady's family, before you married her ?

Belv. Yes : her family and fortune are elegant. She has a guardian, whose address the sweet Obstinate refused to give me, that she might herself reveal the marriage;—which I had reasons, however, to request her not to do, till we both arrived in England.

Fitz. Then you have not seen your bride in England ?

Belv. Oh no !—My *Julia* is yet in her convent. I have been preparing for her reception in Berkshire, and have written to inform her, that I would meet her at Calais; but

I fear my letters have miffed her, and fhall therefore fet out for Paris, to conduct to England the woman who muft give the point to all my felicities.

Fitz. (afide) And has *Julia* been capable of this ?——Ungrateful girl! is it thus fhe rewards my cares?

Belv. Your filence and your refentment, my dear friend, whilft they flatter, diftrefs me.

Fitz. I'm indeed offended at your marriage, but not with you :—on *you* I had no claims.

Belv. I do not apprehend you.

Fitz. Perhaps not ; and at prefent I fhall not explain myfelf. *(going)*

Belv. If you *will* leave me, adieu! I am going to run over the Town. My mind, impatient for the moment which carries me to my fweet bride, feels all the intermediate time a void, which any adventure may fill up. [*Exit.*

Fitz. Spite of my difpleafure, I can hardly conceal from him his happinefs!—Yet I *will.*—*Julia* muft be punifhed. To vice and folly I am content to appear fevere; but *fhe* ought not to have thought me fo. I have not deferved this want of confidence, and muft correct it. If I don't miftake, *Pendragon* is a fit inftrument.—I'll take him home with me. —Yes, yes, my young Lady, you fhall have a lover!— Oh thefe headftrong girls!   [*Exit.*

END OF THE SECOND ACT.

30 Minutes -

Table & Chairs.

2.

ACT III. SCENE I.

LORD SPARKLE'S.

LH   RH

LORD SPARKLE *and* BEAUCHAMP *discover'd at a Table,
on which are Pens, Paper, &c.* SPARKLE *superbly drest.*

Spark. POOR *George!* and so thou wilt really be in a
few days in the bosom of the Atlantic!
" Farewel to green fields and sweet groves,
" Where Chloe engag'd my fond heart."——
(rises and comes forward)
Hey for counterscarps, wounds, and victory!

Beauch. I accept your last words for my omen; and
now, in the true spirit of Homer's Heroes, should take my
congé, and depart, with its influence upon me. ✗ L

Spark. First take an office which I know must charm
you.—You admire Lady *Bell Bloomer?*

Beauch. Admire her!—Yes, by Heaven——*(with great
warmth)*

Spark. (interrupting) No heroics, dear *George*—no heroics! They are totally out now—totally out both in
love and war.

Beauch. How, my Lord!

Spark. Indifference!—that's the rule.—We love, hate,
quarrel, and even fight without suffering our tranquility
to be incommoded;—nothing disturbs.—The keenest discernment will discover nothing particular in the behaviour
of *lovers* on the point of marriage, nor in the *married,*
whilst the articles of separation are preparing.

Beauch. Disgustful apathy!——What becomes of the
energies of the heart in this wretched system? Does it
annihilate your feelings?

Spark. Oh, no!—I feel, for instance, that I must have
Lady *Bell Bloomer,* and I feel curiosity to know her sentiments of me, of which, however, I have very little doubt:
but all my art can't make her serious; she fences admira-
bly, and keeps me at the length of her foil.—To you she
will be less on her guard.

Beauch. Me! you surprise me, my Lord! How can I
be of use in developing her Ladyship's sentiments?

Spark. Why, by sifting them. When you talk of me,
see if she blushes. Mention some woman as one whom I
admire,

admire, and obferve if fhe does not make fome fpiteful re-
mark on her fhape, complexion, or conduct; provoke her
to abufe me with violence, or to fpeak of me with confufion—in either cafe, I have her.

Beauch. Your inftructions are ample, my Lord; but I
do not feel myfelf equal to the embafly.

Spark. *(with pique)* Your pardon, Sir! You *refufe* then
to oblige me?

Beauch. I cannot *refufe* you—my obligations to your
Lordfhip make it impoffible:—but, of all mankind, I perhaps am the laft you fhou'd have chofen for the purpofe.

Spark. Nay, prithee don't be ridiculous! It is the laft
fervice you can do me: and you are the only man whom I
could entruft with fo delicate a bufinefs.

Beauch. I accept it as a proof of your Lordfhip's confidence, and will difcharge the commiffion faithfully.——
(afide) It will at leaft give me an occafion to converfe with
Lady *Bell*, and to converfe with her on *love*.——Oh! my
heart! how wilt thou contain thy ardors in the trying
moment?   *LH* [*Exit* Beauchamp.

Spark. Ha! ha! ha! I am confirm'd in my fufpicions,
that the fellow has had the vanity to indulge a paffion for
Lady *Bell* himfelf. Well, fo much the better! the commiffion I have given him will fufficiently punifh him for his
prefumption.

LH Enter a SERVANT.

Serv. Mrs. *Kitty* is below, my Lord, Mifs *Manners's*
woman.   *LH*

Spark. Ha! Send her up—fend her up. (*Exit* Serv.) I had
began to give up that affair; but I think I won't neither.
It will be rather a brilliant thing to have Lady *Bell* for a
wife, and her friend for a miftrefs:—yes, it will be a
point. I think I'll have the *eclat* of the thing.—*(Enter
Kitty)*—Well, *Kitty*, what intelligence from the land of
intrigue? What fays the little froft-piece *Julia?*

Kitty. Oh, nothing new, my Lord! She's as infenfible
as ever.—I makes orations all day long of your Lordfhip's
merit, and goodnefs, and fondnefs, and——

Spark. *(flaring)* Merit, and *goodnefs*, and *fondnefs!*
And don't you give a parenthefis to my fobriety, and my
neatnefs too! Ha! ha! ha! you foolifh little devil, I
thought you knew better!—Tell her of my fafhion, my
extravagance; that I play deepeft at ~~Welljie's~~, am the beft-
dreft

$$\overline{}\\ 3.$$

Mr. Heath. Cooper

·

dreſt at the Opera, and have half ruined myſelf by grant-
ing annuities to pretty girls.——Goodneſs and fondneſs are
baits to catch old prudes, not blooming miſſes.

Kitty. What, my Lord! is ſpreading out your faults
the way to win a fair Lady?

Spark. Faults! Thine is chambermaid's morality, with
a vengeance!—What have all my paſt leſſons been thrown
away upon thee, Innocence!—Have I not told thee, that
the governing paſſion of the female mind is the rage of
being envied? The moſt generous of them wou'd like to
break the hearts of half-a-dozen of their friends, by the
preference given to themſelves. Go home again, good
Kitty, and con your leſſon afreſh: if you can pick up any
ſtories of extravagance and gallantry, affix my name to
'em and repeat them to your miſtreſs.

Kitty. Then ſhe'll tell 'em to Lady *Bell,* perhaps, for a
warning——

Spark. (drawling) For a warning, quotha!—My devoirs to Lady *Bell* are of a different kind, and we underſtand each other. I addreſs *her* for a wife, becauſe ſhe's
the faſhion; and I addreſs *Julia* for a miſtreſs, becauſe 'tis
the faſhion to have miſtreſſes from higher orders than ſemp-
ſtreſſes and mantua-makers.

Kitty. And is that your only reaſon, my Lord, for
bribing me ſo high?

Spark. Not abſolutely. I have a pique againſt her
guardian, who, tho' he has the honour to be related to me,
will not ſuffer me to draw on his banker for a ſingle gui-
nea. His eſtates, indeed, he can't deprive me of; ſo as it
can do no harm, I'll have the *eclat* of affronting him with
ſpirit.

Kitty. Oh Gemini! I am glad to hear that! I'd do
any thing to plague Mr. *Fitzherbert,* and can go on now
with a ſafe conſcience!—He had like to have loſt me my
place once, becauſe he thought I was flighty;—but I'll be
up with him, now.

LH Enter SERVANT.

Serv. Mr. *Belville.*   [*Exit LH*

LH Enter BELVILLE.

Spark. My dear *Belville! (apart)* Go, *Kitty,* into that
room, I'll ſpeak to you preſently.   [*Exit* Kitty. *RH*
                                                           Welcome

Welcome once more to the region of bu
fure!

Belv. I thank you! But pray, my Lord
the lady.

Spark. The lady! Ha! ha! ha! That
Lady's *gentlewoman*, a'n't pleafe ye! I fup
heard that I am going to marry Lady *Bell B*
the two moft fafhionable people in town
muft come together.

Belv. A clear deduction.

Spark. Now fhe has a friend, whom I m
time to take for a miftrefs:—won't that be

Belv. Decidedly. ~~Your life is made~~
Every thing with you, my Lord, is a hit.

Spark. True, true! I deteft a regular m
of doing things.—Men of fenfe have one
through life; men of genius, another.

Belv. Doubtlefs; and the advantage lie
of genius, for to their *genius* are all their
nay, their faults are confidered as the grace
of a mind *too ethereal* to be confined to the
mon-fenfe and decorum;—a mighty eafy v
reputation! ha! ha! ha! ~~You are dref
malice to-day, my Lord.~~

Spark. Malice! Not at all.—The wom
~~are neither~~ caught by finery or perfon!—
~~court~~—I was going to Weftminfter; but
to be a prefentation of *Miffes* to-day, and I
the world lofe the dear creatures blufhes o
pearance; for, faith, moft of them will ne
—Will you go?

Belv. 'Tis too late to drefs: befides, I h
day to adventure. I am rambling through
covering what new ftars have appeared in
Beauty during my abfence, and a dangerou
The rays of a pair of black eyes from a
mall would have annihilated me, had not
ftant two beautiful blue ones from a windo
to my finking fpirits. A fine turn'd ancl
fhone through its neat filk ftocking, enc
St. James's-ftreet; but I was luckily reli
rofy mouth, that betray'd, with a deceitf
moft murderoufly white. A Galatea darte
right, whilft a Helen fwam along on the
from fuch fweet befiegers nothing could ha

4.

1.

but what is to be done? when we
want the supplies, we must raise
the rents. 'Adieu.'

Exit Lt.

but the fweeter charms of a beloved, though abfent fair-
one. *(fighing)*

Spark. Now, I never trouble my head about abfentees !
—I love beauty as well as any man ; but it muft be all in
the prefent tenfe. Shall I fet you down any where ? I
muft go. X *L.*

Belv. No ; but I fee your writing things are here. If
you'll permit me, I'll pen a fhort note to *Beauchamp* on
bufinefs I had forgot this morning, and difpatch it by a
chairman.

Spark. To be fure. I penned a note ten minutes fince to
my fteward, to raife the poor devils rents. Upon my foul,
I pity 'em ! But how can it be otherwife, whilft one is
obliged to wear fifty acres in a fuit, and the produce of a
whole farm in a pair of buckles ? Adieu ! *[Exit finging.* L.H

*(Whilft Sparkle is fpeaking, Belville feats himfelf, and begins
to write.)*

Belv. *(writing)* Good morning !—My compliments to
the Ladies bluflies.

R.H *Enter* KITTY ; *paffes* BELVILLE *in the front of the Stage.*

Kitty. So, fo, his Lordfhip has forgot me ! I muft go
after him.

Belv. *(coming forward)* Hah ! that's the confidante !—
So pretty-one, whofe chattels are you ?

Kitty. My miftrefs's, Sir.

Belv. And who is your miftrefs ?

Kitty. A Lady, Sir.

Belv. And her name ?

Kitty. That of her father, I take it.

Belv. Upon my word, your Lady has a very brilliant
fervant !—Is fhe as clever as you are ?

Kitty. Why, not quite, I think, or fhe would not keep
me to eclipfe her.

Belv. Bravo ! I wifh I knew her ! Will you tell me her
name ?

Kitty. Can you fpell ?

enough who me is.—I heard you the here speak asking
about her. Let me go ; for I am going to carry a meſſage
to Mr. *Fitzherbert*.

Belv. Mr. *Fitzherbert!*

Kitty. Aye, her guardian.

Belv. Her guardian! What, *Fitzherbert* of Cambridge-
ſhire ?

Kitty. Yes; and if you want to know more, he's the
croſſeſt old wretch that ever breathed. You'll find him
out by that deſcription ; and ſo, your ſervant ! [*Exit* Kitty. *LH*

Belv. *Fitzherbert*'s ward ! and this creature her ſervant !
and Lord *Sparkle* plotting to get her for a miſtreſs !—I am
aſtoniſh'd !—the *very* Lady he this morning offered for my
bride !——Well,—I muſt find *Fitzherbert* immediately.——
Lord *Sparkle* will perhaps think me guilty of a breach of
honour—The *imputation* I muſt incur, that I may not be
really guilty of a breach of humanity, and of gratitude.

[*Exit* Belville. *LH*

SCENE II. *Lady* BELL BLOOMER's. 2ᵈG-

LH Enter FITZHERBERT, *followed by a Servant.*

Fitz. Tell Miſs *Manners* I am here. (*Exit* Servant.)— *RH*
I cannot perhaps be ſeriouſly angry with *Julia* ; but I muſt
take ſome revenge on her diſobedience, before I acquaint
her with the felicity that attends her. Come in, Young
Corniſh, pray !

LH Enter PENDRAGON.

Pen. What, does the Lady live in this fine houſe ?

Fitz. Yes :—but pray obſerve, that I don't engage ſhe
ſhall be *ſmitten* with you. I can go no farther than to introduce you ; the reſt muſt depend on the brilliancy of your
manners.

Pen. Oh leave me alone for that !—I knew how 'twould
be, if I once ſhew'd myſelf in London. If ſhe has a long
purſe, I'll whiſk her down to Cornwall, jockey Lord
Sparkle, and have the Borough myſelf.

Fitz. A man of ſpirit, I ſee !

Pen. Oh, as to my ſpirit, that nobody ever doubted !—
I have beat our Exciſeman, and gone to law with the Par-
ſon ; and to ſhew you that I did not leave my ſpirit in the

Clear Stage –

Pink Chair & G.

Mr. ~~Sutton~~   Chairs –   Mr. Addis

country, since I came to London I have fined a hackney-
coachman for abuse.

Fitz. Very commendable!—But here comes the Lady!

RH Enter JULIA.

Mr. *Pendragon*, this is my ward, who, I am sure, will
give your addresses all the encouragement I wish them.

Pen. Servant, Ma'am! *(aside)* She looks plaguy glum.

R Julia. I can scarcely support myself! *(aside)*

C Fitz. Pray, my dear, speak to Mr. *Pendragon!* You
seem greatly confused!

Pen. Oh, Sir, I understand it! Young Ladies will
look confus'd and embarrass'd, and all that sort of thing,
on these occasions; but we men of the world are up to all
that.

R Julia. Heavens! is it to such a Being I should have
been sacrificed! *(aside)*

L Pen. I see your ward is one of the modest diffident ones:
I am surprised at that—bred in high-life.

C Fitz. Oh, now and then, you find a person of that cast
in the best company!—but they soon get over it.

Pen. Yes, formerly I used to blush, and be modest, and
all that sort of thing; but if any one ever catches me modest
again, I'll give 'em my estate for a pilchard.

Julia. Then it seems impossible——pardon me, Sir! *(to
Fitzherbert)* that a union can take place between you and
me; for I place modesty amongst the *elegancies* of manners,
and think it absolutely necessary to the character of a gentleman.

Fitz. Well done, *Julia! (aside)*—Fye upon you to treat
my friend with such asperity!

Pen. O leave her to me, Sir; she's ignorant, but I shall
teach her. There are three things, Miss, only necessary
to the character of a Gentleman; a good air, good assurance, and good teeth. *(grinning)*

Julia. (to Fitzherbert) Doesn't his list want *good manners,* Sir?

ur hufband, you lose *me.*—Keep it

it for you below, *(to* Pendragon).-

ce and difobedience correct each oth

[Exit

w to ftrike her with my fuperior *ca*

your Guardian, I think, has a m

he vulgar fpeech—marry! *(Sits*

Well, Sir; but are you not frigh

q fuch a ftate!—Do you know wh

er of a Hufband?

'hat belongs to it?. Aye! Do you

being a Wife?

Yes; I guefs that to *your* wife wi

ith you at home—fhame with you

re'd fmiles—in her heart hidden th

he Devil! What, you have found

Oh, oh, I fhall have a fine time c

connection begins!

Our connection!—Pray, Sir, drop

to you, that were it poffible for m

, I fhould be the moft wretched of v

h no, you woudn't! I hardly knov

ched.

Unfeeling man! Would *you* prefu

e, to the happinefs of which, union

ntiment, and all the elegant attentic

are neceffary and indifpenfible?

/hat's all that! Union of foul! fe

—That's not Life, I'm fure.

I am not able to conceive by wh

erbert has been blinded to the weal

the turpitude of your heart.—T

ot a fate I would not prefer to that of

whofe vice is the effect of folly, an

ful even as his vice.

'es, yes, I'll tell, depend on't!—I

fo much the better, more pleafure in

k wife cheats a man of his rights,

he pleafure of *exacting* her obedience

Vice—folly—impudence—ignoranc

[Ex

6.

7.

Kitty puts back Chairs.

Clear Stage

Julia. What have I done ? I dare not now fee
dian! His difpleafure will kill me. Oh *Belvi.*
art thou! Come and fhield thy unhappy bride
fteps can I take!

RH Enter KITTY.

Kitty. Dear Ma'am, I'm fo griev'd to fee you
py! If I had fuch a crofs old guardian, I'd run a
him.

Julia. The very thought which that inftant
itfelf to my mind!—Have you not told me, tha
lation of your's has lodgings?

Kitty. Yes, Ma'am; the moft eleganteft in Lo

Julia. I don't want elegant apartments; but
a fhort time to be conceal'd in fome family of rep

Kitty. To be fure, Ma'am, 'tis the moft pru
you can do.

Julia. And yet my heart fails me.

Kitty. Oh, Ma'am, don't hefitate! I'll go and
few things, and call a coach and be off, before
comes from Court.

Julia. I fear 'tis a wrong ftep; and yet what
take? I dare not reveal my marriage, without
miffion of my hufband; and till his arrival, I
both a guardian's anger and the addreffes of a
The honour of *Belville* would be infulted, fhoul
them to be repeated. *(afide)*

Kitty. I know not what fhe means, but the
myftery, I find. So there fhould be!——If ladi
myfteries, a chamber-maid's place would be ha
keeping.——I have myfteries too, and fhe fhall
explanation from Lord *Sparkle.*

SCENE III. CLARINDA'S *Houfe*

RH Enter Lady BELL *meeting* CLARIND

L. Bell. Ha! ha! ha! my dear creature, wh
barras! Driving fwiftly through the ftreets, La
cord dafh'd upon us in her flaming phæton and
monftrous big Newmarket word to my poor fel

with infinite dexterity entangled the traces. It happen'd near your door; so I have taken shelter with you, and left her Ladyship to settle the dispute with my coachman, ha! ha! ha! But why were you not at Court to-day?

Clar. I had a teazing head-ach; but pray, tell me what happen'd there.—*(aside)* Deuce take her, she looks as well as ever!

L. Bell. Oh, the Ladies, as usual, brilliant—nothing so flat as the men! The horrid *English* custom ruins them for conversation. They make themselves members of Clubs, in the way of business; and Members of Parliament, in the way of amusement: all their passions are reserved for the first, and all their wit for the last.

Clar. 'Tis better in Paris.

L. Bell. Oh, 'tis quite another thing! Whilst we aukwardly copy the follies of the Parisians, we absurdly omit the charming part of their character. Devoted to elegance, they catch their opinions, their wit, and their bon mots from the mouths of the ladies.—'Tis in the drawing-room of Madame the Dutchess, the Marquis learns his politicks; whilst the sprightly Countess dispenses taste and philosophy to a circle of Bishops, Generals, and Abbés.

Clar. All that may be just; yet I am mistaken, if you have not found *one* Englishman to reconcile you to the manners of the rest. Lord *Sparkle*, for instance—your Ladyship thinks, I'm sure, that *he* has wit at will.

L. Bell. Oh yes, quite at will!——His wit, like his essence-bottle, is a collection of all that is poignant in a thousand flowers; and, like that, is most useful, when he himself is most insipidly vacant.

Clar. With such sentiments, I wonder you can suffer his addresses.

L. Bell. What *can* I do? The man is so much the fashion, and I shall be so much envied.——Why you know, my dear, for instance—you'd be inclin'd to stick a poisoned nosegay in my bosom, if I should take him.

Clar. Ha! ha! ha! ridiculous! Believe me, Madam, I shall neither prepare a bouquet, nor invoke a fiery shower to grace your nuptials.

L. Bell. *(aside)* No, your showers would be tears, I fancy.——Here he comes!

Clar. Hah! Lord *Sparkle!* Your Ladyship's accident was fortunate. *(sneering)*

Enter

R. a. B.

Wm Keath.

lus. I follow'd you from St. James's

h-born cattle wouldn't keep pace with
 don't complain! If her Ladyſhip v
 ſhe ſtopp'd for you at the goal.
arming Miſs *Belmour*, what an enliv'
 'here was your Ladyſhip on Th
 ave found excellent food for your
 We had all the Law Ladies from L
 1 gold velvets from Biſhopſgate, v
 ughters of half the M. D's. and LL

)h, my entertainment was quite as
were in Brook-ſtreet, at Lady *Laur*
 rounded by her Literati of all denom
 I Maſters of Art and Miſſes of Scien
 an Eſſayiſt; on the other, a Moral
 after; here, a Tranſlator :——in tha
 r: in the other, a compiler of M:
 Epigrams, and Syllogiſms flew l
ery direction; 'till the ambition of
d the flame of controverſy, when t
 he *lye literary* with infinite ſpirit and d
cellent! I'll repeat every word in
 be remember'd, and the ſatire enjoy'
that hope your Lordſhip may ſafely
 1 the ſtreet :—ſatire is welcome every
 'es, if it will bear a laugh—that's t
ſation. They pretend we are fond of
 lal of its laugh, and 'twould ſoon be
d table, for the amuſement of but
ds.
deed! Then I believe half our acq
 own ſtairs to the ſecond table too!—
 ervants had the beſt of the diſh. (*En*
 Lord Sparkle *a letter, and exit.*) *R H*
 ads it aſide) *Julia!* aſtoniſhing!—S
 ements, Mrs. *Kitty?*—(*turning to th*
 thing call'd buſineſs is the greateſt ev
 our moſt brilliant hours, and is fit
 thers and humble couſins.——Miſs B
 rſelf away. Shall I attend your La
 ?

. Shine upon you at night!—That I know you are
t enough to believe impoffible.—What can I think
fentiments for Lord *Sparkle!* Sometimes I believe
here attachment of vanity on both fides.—That re-
creature *Beauchamp* is in his confidence; but he
town this very day, and I fhall have no opportunity
erfing with him. *(mufes)* There is but one chance—
to vifit him.——But how can I poffibly do that?
take him! If he had a library, one might go to look
books. Well, I don't care, go I will; and if I can't
an excufe, I'll put a good face upon the matter,
without one.—*(going)* I fhould expire if my vifit
be difcover'd. Poh! I muft rifque every thing!—
bold, is fometimes to be right. [*Exit.*

ND OF THE THIRD ACT.

32 Minutes.

Chap. 6. 3.9

[signature]

ACT IV. SCENE I.

An Apartment at LADY BELL's.

LH Enter LADY BELL, *followed by her* ~~Maid.~~ *Servt.*

L. Bell. MISS *Manners* gone out in a hackney-coach, and no meſſage left!

Maid. No, Madam.

L. Bell. Very ſtrange!

Maid. Mr. *Beauchamp* has been waiting almoſt an hour for your Ladyſhip's return.

L. Bell. Mr. *Beauchamp!*—Here, go and put ſome otto of roſes in that handkerchief. (*Exit* ~~Servt~~) Now, ſhall I admit him, or not? This formal waiting looks very like formal buſineſs. Poh, I hate that!—I ſuppoſe he has at length vanquiſh'd his modeſty, and is come to tell me that—that—Well, I vow I won't hear him.—Yes, I will. I long to know the ſtile in which theſe reſerv'd men make love.—To what imprudence would my heart betray me? Yet I may ſurely indulge myſelf in hearing him *ſpeak* of love; in hearing, probably for the firſt time, its genuine language. (*Enter Servt. and preſents the handkerchief*) Tell Mr. *Beauchamp* I am here. (*Exit Servt.*) Now, how ſhall I receive him? It will be intolerable to be formal.—(*Takes her fan from her pocket and traverſes the ſtage, humming a tune.—Enter* Beauchamp.) Oh, Mr. *Beauchamp*, this is the luckieſt thing!—I have had ten diſputes to-day about the figures in my fan; and you ſhall decide 'em. Is that beautiful nymph a flying Daphne, or an Atalanta?

Beauch. (*looking at her fan*) From the terror of the eye, Madam, and the ſwiftneſs of her ſtep, it muſt be a Daphne. I think Atalanta's head would be more at variance with her feet; and whilſt ſhe *flies,* her eye would be invitingly turn'd on her purſuers.

L. Bell. I think you are right!—Yes—there does want the kind, inviting glance, to be ſure.

Beauch. What a misfortune to a lover! I know one to whom your Ladyſhip appears the diſdainful Daphne.—— How happy! could he behold in *your* eye the encourage-ment of Atalanta's!

L. Bell. (aside) Mercy! for fo bafhful a man that's pretty plain.

Beauch. This is probably the laft-vifit I can make you before I leave England :—will your Ladyfhip permit me, *before* I leave it, to acquaint you that there is a man, whofe happinefs depends on your favour? *(agitated)*

L. Bell. So, now he's going to be perplexing again! *(aside)*—A man whofe happinefs depends on me, Mr. Beauchamp! *(looking on her fan)*

Beauch. Yes, Madam!—and—and—*(aside)* I cannot go on——Why did I accept a commiffion in which fuccefs would deftroy me?

L. Bell. How evidently this is the firft time he ever made love! *(aside)*—The man feems to have chofen a very diffident advocate in you, Sir.

Beauch. 'Tis *more* than diffidence, Madam, my tafk is painful.

L. Bell. Ay, I thought fo! You have taken a brief in a caufe you don't like; I could plead it better myfelf.

Beauch. I feel the reproach.

L. Bell. 'Tis difficult for you, perhaps, to fpeak in the *third* perfon?——Try it in the *firft*. Suppofe now, ha! ha! only fuppofe, I fay! for the jeft's fake, that you yourfelf have a paffion for me, and *then* try—how you can plead it.

Beauch. (kneeling) Thus—thus would I plead it, and fwear, that thou art dear to my heart as fame, and honour!—To look at thee is rapture; to love thee, though without hope,—felicity!

L. Bell. Oh, I thought I fhould bring him to the point at laft! *(aside)*

Beauch. (rifing, afide) To what difhonefty have I been betray'd!—Thus, Madam, fpeaks my friend, through my lips;—'tis thus *he* pleads his paffion.

L. Bell. Provoking! *(aside)*—*What* friend is this, Sir, who is weak enough to ufe the language of another to explain his heart?

Beauch. Lord *Sparkle.*

L. Bell. Lord *Sparkle!* Was it for him you knelt? *(he bows to her)*—Then, Sir, I muft inform you, that the liberty you have taken——*(aside)* Heavens, how do I betray myfelf!—Tell me, Sir, on your honour, do you *wifh* to fucceed in pleading the paffion of Lord *Sparkle?*

                                                   Beauch.

2.

x x
 x   *Ready to Knock L.*

Chairs. *Swedish Chair*

3.

×××

Beauch. (*hesitating*) My obligations to his Lordship——our relationship—the confidence he has repos'd in me—

L. Bell. Stop, Sir! I too will repose confidence in you, and confess that there is a man whom I sometimes suspect not to be indifferent to me;—but 'tis not Lord *Sparkle!* Tell him so;—and tell him that—that—tell him what you will.

Beauch. Heavens, what does she mean! What language is this her eye speaks? (*aside*) [*He bows*]

L. Bell. Do you visit me this evening? Here will be many of my friends, and you shall then see me in the presence of the man my heart prefers.

(Beauchamp *bows, and goes to the door; then returns, advances towards Lady Bell, makes an effort to speak; finds it impossible, then bows, and exit.*) *LH*

Heavens! what necessity have lovers for words? What persuasion in that bashful irresolution! Now, shall I let him quit England, or not!—What! give up a coronet and Lord *Sparkle* for a cockade and *Beauchamp!* Preposterous! says Vanity.—But what says Love? I don't exactly know; but I'll examine their separate claims, and settle them with all the casuistry of four-and-twenty.

[*Exit.* RH

SCENE II. Lord SPARKLE's *House.*

LH Enter JULIA *and* KITTY.

Julia. I am so agitated with this rash step, that I can hardly breathe! (*throwing herself into a chair*) Why did you confirm me in my imprudent resolution?

Kitty. Imprudent! I'm sure, Ma'am, 'tis very prudent, and very right, that a young lady like you should not be snubb'd, and have her inclination thwarted by an ill-natur'd positive old guardian.

Julia. (*looking round*) What apartments! and the hall we came through had an air much beyond a lodging-house! 'Tis all too fine for my purpose; I want to be private.

Kitty. Oh dear Ma'am, you may be as private here as you please! (*a rapping at the door*) There's my cousin come home, I dare say; I'll send her to you, and then you may settle terms. [*Exit.* LH

Julia. I feel I have done wrong, and yet I am so distracted, I know not how I could have done otherwise.

H (*Enter* Lord Sparkle) Heavens! Lord *Sparkle* here!

F 2

Spark.

Spark. Yes, my lovely *Julia*, here I am; and upon my foul, if you knew the engagements I have broke for the happiness, you would be gratified.

Julia. Gratified! I am aftonish'd! equally aftonish'd at your being here, and at your ftrange addrefs.

Spark. Aftonish'd at my being here! Why, to be fure, it is not ufual to find a man of fashion in his own houfe; but when I heard that you were in my houfe, how could I do lefs than fly home?

Julia. Home! Your own houfe! What can all this mean?—

Spark. Mean! Love—Gallantry—Joy, and ever-new delights.

Julia. Oh! I am betray'd! Where is my wicked fervant?

Spark. Poh, never think of her!—Why all this flutter, my fweet girl! You have only chang'd guardians; and you fhall find, that being ward to a young man of fashion and fpirit, is a very different thing from——

Julia. Oh Heavens! what will become of me?

Spark. Nay, this is quite ridiculous, after having fled to my protection! I feel myfelf highly honour'd by your confidence, and will take care to deferve it.

Julia. Why do I remain here an inftant?

(going towards the door)

Spark. (*holding her*) This is downright rudenefs! But you young Ladies are fo fickle in your refolutions—But be affured, after having chofen my houfe for your afylum, I fhall not be fo impolite as to fuffer you to feek another.

Julia. Oh wretched artifice! You know, Sir, that your houfe and *you* I would have fled from to the fartheft corner of—*I.H.*—(*Enter* Beauchamp) Oh, Mr. *Beauchamp*, fave me!—I have been bafely betray'd!—

Beauch. (*aftonish'd*) Betray'd!—Mifs *Manners*! Yes, Madam, I will protect you at every hazard. */Puts her over*

Spark. Come, none of your antique virtues, *George*, pray! This is a piece of *badinage* of the Eighteenth Century, and you can't poffibly underftand it!—Mifs *Manners* chofe to pay me a vifit, and I defire you'll leave us.

Julia. My Lord, how dare you thus trifle with a woman's honor?

Beauch. Be not alarm'd, Madam, I will defend you.

Spark. (*taking him afide*) Poh, prithee, *George*, be difcreet! This is all female artifice!—You popp'd upon us, and this is a falver for her reputation.

D......l.

4.

Copper

Beauch. Pardon me, my Lord! In believing you, in op-
pofition to the evidence of this young Lady's terrors, I
may be guilty of an irremiable error.

Spark. Nay, if you are ferious, Sir, how dare you break
in upon my privacy?

Beauch. This is not a time to anfwer you, my Lord!
The bufinefs that brought me here, I am indebted to; I
fhould not elfe have prevented your bafe defigns.

Spark. Bafe defigns, Mr. *Beauchamp!*

Beauch. Yes, Lord *Sparkle!*—Shall I attend you home,
Madam?

Julia. Oh, Sir, I dare not go there! I fled from Lady
Bell's, when I was betray'd into this inhuman man's power.—Convey me to fome place where I may have leifure to
reflect.

Spark. And do you think, Mr. *Beauchamp*, I fhall put
up with this!—Remember, Sir——

Beauch. (interrupting) Yes, my Lord, that, as a *Man*,
it is my duty to protect endanger'd innocence; that, as a
Soldier, it is part of the effence of my character; and,
whilft I am grateful to you for the commiffion I have the
honour to bear, I will not difgrace it, in fuffering myfelf
to be intimidated by your frowns. [*Exit* Beauchamp, *leading*
Julia.] *LH*

Spark. So!—fo!—fo!—an antient hero in the houfe of
a modern man of fafhion!—Alexander in the tent of Da-
rius!—Scipio and the fair Parthenia! The fellow has not
an idea of any morals but thofe in ufe during the
Olympiads.

LH Enter SERVANT.

Serv. Mr. *Pendragon* and his fifter, my Lord.

Spark. Who! *(with an air of difguft)*

Serv. Mr. and Mifs *Pendragon.*

Spark. Then carry 'em to the Houfekeeper's room!——
Give 'em jellies and plumb-cake, and tell 'em—*(Enter* Pen- *LH*
dragon, *leading* Sophy) Oh, my dear Mifs *Pendragon*, you
honour me!—But I am the moft unlucky man on earth!—
I am oblig'd, upon bufinefs of infinite confequence, to be

Sophy. Well, now you talk of being miserable, you have soften'd my heart at once! But pray, my Lord, is it fashionable for people on the terms you and I are, to keep asunder?

Spark. What the Devil can the girl mean? *(aside)*

Sophy. Never even write!—no billets!—no bribing the maid to flip notes into my hand!——Why you don't even complain, tho' 'tis five days since you saw me.

Spark. Complain! I am sure I have been exceedingly wretched.

Sophy. Then why did you not tell me so? Why, that's the very thing I wanted! If I had known you had been wretched, I should have been happy.

Pen. Well, I see I shall lose an opportunity here!—I came to challenge you, my Lord.

Spark. Challenge me!

Pen. Yes!—Miss *Pendragon* told me she was *diffatisfied*:——then says I, *I'll* demand *fatisfaction*:——and I didn't care if things had gone a little farther; for to call out a Lord would be a feather in my cap as long as I live.—— However, you are agreed.

Sophy. Do be quiet, *Bobby!*—We are not agreed:—I have heard nothing of Settlements yet; nothing of Jewels.

Spark. My dear Ma'am, you are pleas'd to amuse yourself.

Sophy. Why, my Lord, those things must be all settled before-hand, you know.

Spark. Before what!

Sophy. What! Before our marriage, my Lord.

Spark. Marriage! Ha! ha! ha!

Sophy. Hey-dey! Will you pretend that you did not intend to marry me, when I can prove that you have courted me from twenty instances?

Spark. Indeed!

Pen. Ay, that she can! instances as striking as your

5.

said, " *I was a most bewitching and adorable girl!*"—exactly what Colonel Finch said to Lady Lucy Lustre!—Another time you said, " *How would a' Coronet become those
shining tresses!*"—the very speech of Lord Rosehill to Miss
Danvers ; and these couples were every one married.

Spark. Married! I never heard of 'em!—Who are they?
Where the Devil do they live ?

Pen. (strutting up to him) Live ?—Why in our county,
to be sure.

Sophy. No, no, *Bobby*, in *The Reclaim'd Rake*, and *The
Constant Lovers*, and *Sir Charles Grandison*, and *Roderick
Random*, and——

Pen. Yes, Sir; they live at Random, with Sir Charles
Grandison.—Now d'ye know 'em ?

Spark. Ha! ha! ha! you are a charming little Lawyer,
(to Sophy) and might, perhaps, establish your proofs for
precedents, if Sir Charles Grandison was on the Bench :
yet I never heard of his being made Chief Justice, tho' I
never thought him fit for any thing else.

Pen. What the Devil's this ?——What, did not you
bring all those fine proofs from fashionable life ?—And are
you such a fool as not to understand what we call *common-
place ?*

Sophy. Common-place!

Pen. Yes, we persons of elegant life use the figure
Hyperbole.——

Sophy. Hyperbole! What's that ?

Pen. Why, that's as much as to say, a stretch.

Sophy. A stretch! What, then, you have been mocking
me, my Lord ?

Spark. Not in the least; I shall be the happiest man ex-
isting to, to—*(aside)* Egad, I must take care of my phrases!
——I mean that I shall be always, and upon all occasions,
your most devoted, *tres humble serviteur*.——Were
there ever two such Bumpkins! *[Exit.*

Sophy. What's he gone ? Oh! Villain! Monster! I
am forsaken! Oh! I am rejected!——All Cornwall will
know it! *(crying)*

that fort of thing; and whether *for* ye or *againft* ye, 'twill be much the fame.'

Sophy. But will you challenge him, really, *Bobby?*

Pen. Upon honor!———I admire the *claw* of the thing! Egad, *Sophy*, I'm glad he's forfaken thee! Now my cha-racter will be finifh'd. A man can't fhew his face in com-pany, till he has ftood fhot, and fired his piftol in the air.

Sophy. In the air! If you don't fire it *thro'* him——

Pen. Oh, never fear! I'll do all that fort of thing. Come along! I'll go home directly, and practife at the hen--coop in the yard. I'll fire through one end, and you fhall hold your calafh againft the other; and if I don't hit it, fay I'm no markfman.

[*Exit* Pendragon, *with* Sophy *under his arm.* **LE**

SCENE III. BEAUCHAMP'S *Lodgings.*

RH Enter Beauchamp *and* Julia.

Beauch. I intreat your pardon for conducting you to my own lodgings;—but here, Madam, you will be fafe, 'till you determine how to act.—What are your commands for me?

Julia. Oh, Mr. *Beauchamp*, I have no commands—I have no defigns!—I have been very imprudent; I am ftill more unhappy.

Beauch. Shall I acquaint Mr. *Fitzherbert?*

Julia. It was to avoid him that I left Lady *Bell.*—I have reafons that make it impoffible to fee Mr. *Fitzherbert* now.

Beauch. Is there no other friend?

Julia. O yes, I have *one* friend!—Were he here, all my difficulties would vanifh!—It may feem ftrange, Mr. *Beauchamp*, but I expect that you believe—Heavens! here's company! (*looking at the wing*) 'Tis Mifs *Belmour*—the laft woman on earth whom I would truft!—Where can I go?

Beauch. Mifs *Belmour!* Very odd!—But pray be not uneafy?—That room, Madam, if you will condefcend—(*fhe rufhes thro' the door.*) Centre

RH Enter CLARINDA *laughing.*

Clar. Ha! ha! ha! I expect your gravity to be amazing-ly difcompos'd at fo hardy a vifit; but I took it very ill that you did not defign to call upon me before your depar-ture;

Clear Stage   6.

Sofa Chair 2^d.G.

ture; and fo as I was paffing your door, I ftopp'd in mere
frolic to enquire the caufe.

Beauch. You do me infinite honour, Madam! I am thank-
ful that I fail'd in my attention, fince it has procur'd me fo
diftinguifh'd a favour.

Clar. Oh, your moft obedient!—You are going to leave
England for a long while! You'll find us all in different
fituations, probably, on your return!—Your friend Lord
Sparkle, for inftance—I am inform'd that he is really to
marry Lady *Bell Bloomer*; but I don't believe it—do you?

Beauch. 'Tis impoffible, Madam, for me——

Clar. Poh! poh! *impoffible!* Such friends as you are I
fuppofe keep nothing from one another.—We women
can't exift without a confidante; and I dare fay, you men
are full as communicative. Not that it is any thing to me;
but as I have a prodigious regard for Lady *Bell*—

Belv. (*behind*) Beauchamp! Beauchamp!

Clar. Heaven and earth, how unlucky! Here's fome
man! I am the niceft creature breathing in my reputation:
what will he think? I'll run into this room. (*runs toward
the door.*)

Beauch. (*preventing her*) Pardon me, Madam, you cannot enter there!

Clar. (*pufhing at the door*) I muft—Oh—oh! the door
is held, Sir.

Beauch. My dear Madam, I am infinitely forry for the
accident; but fuppofe——fuppofe, I fay, Ma'am, that a
friend of mine has been in a duel, and conceal'd in that
room.

Clar. Ridiculous! I faw ~~the corner of a hoop and~~ a
~~white fattin~~ petticoat:—is that the drefs of your duelling
friends? I will go in.—(*ftruggling*) So! (*flinging away
fpitefully*) 'tis too late!

<u>*RH*</u> *Enter* BELVILLE.

el. So! fo! fo! I beg your pardon. How could you be fo
indifcreet, *Beauchamp?* Tho' a young foldier, I thought
you knew enough of Generalfhip to be prepar'd for a fur-
prize.

Clar. Oh, fo he was; but not for *two* furprizes.—One
has happened already, and a hafty retreat the confequence.

Beauch. Believe me, *Belville*—I am infinitely concerned
(*to* Clarinda.)

Clar.

Clar. Oh! I deteſt your impertinent concern! Keep it for the Lady in the other room.

Bel. A Lady in the other room too! Hey-dey! *Beauchamp*, who would have ſuſpected— ✗ C

Beauch. 'Tis all a miſtake! The Lady in the next room —But prithee go.—

Bel. Only tell me if you have ſeen *Fitzberbert.* I have been ſeeking him this hour, on a buſineſs of the utmoſt conſequence.

Beauch. I have not; but about this time you'll find him at home.

Bel. Enough! Miſs *Belmour*, pray ſuffer no concern; depend on my honour.—*Beauchamp (taking bim aſide)*, who is the Lady in the other room?

Beauch. Had I meant you to have known, that room would have been unneceſſary. (*Belville ſeems ſtill inquiſitive; Beauchamp draws him towards the wing.)*

Clar. Now do I die to know who it can be! Indeed, 'tis neceſſary for my own ſake.—Whilſt *ſhe* has been hid, I have been expoſed; and who knows what the creature may ſay? I'll try once more. She has my ſecret, and I'll have her's. (*forces open the door.)*

Julia. (*ruſhes out*) Belville! (*running towards him.)*

Belv. (*ſtarting back*) *Julia!*

Clar. Miſs *Manners!*—Ha! ha! ha!

Julia. Oh, *Belville*, throw me not from you!

Belv. Aſtoniſhing!

Clar. Oh charming! The modeſt *Julia*, and the reſerv'd *Beauchamp!* Ha! ha! ha!—But Mr. *Belville*, how came *you* of this ſober party? ha! ha! ha!

Julia. Speak to me!

Clar. Now, Mr. *Beauchamp*, you know the purport of my viſit.——I had heard that Miſs *Manners* has been ſeen to viſit you, and, not being willing to truſt to ſuch a report, was reſolved, if poſſible, to diſcover the truth.

Bel. (*to Julia*) Wretched woman! ✗ ʎ

Julia. (*to Clarinda*) Barbarous creature! Oh hear me, I conjure you!

Bel. Hear you!—No, Madam;—and if my contempt, my hatred, my——oh!——*You*, Sir, I muſt ſpeak to in another place;—yet perhaps you were not acquainted that ——What would I ſay!——The word which I have pro-

nounced

7.

R. a. B.

nounced with rapture, choaks me. From this moment
farewel ! *(to Julia)*   [*Exit* Belville.

Beauch. What can I think of all this?

Julia. Oh Sir!

Beauch. Permit me, Madam, to afk if you have long
known Mr. *Belville?*

Julia. Yes, too long.

Clar. Oh, oh, *too* long!—Aye, young ladies fhould be
cautious how they form acquaintance. For my part—But
you look ill, child!—*(taking her by the hand)* Well, I have
no hard heart; I can pity your weaknefs, Mifs;—I won't
upbraid you now.—My coach waits;—fhall I conduct you
home?

Julia. Yes, to Lady *Bell*——to Lady *Bell*——I am very.
ill!

Clar. Adieu, Mr. *Beauchamp!* This has been an unlucky
frolic!—'Tis amazing, you grave people can be fo care-
lefs.   [*Exit* Julia *and* Clarinda.

Beauch. An unlucky frolick, indeed! And I am fo
thoroughly confounded, that I know not what judgment
to form of the adventure.—I always confidered Mifs *Man-*
ners as a pattern of delicacy and virtue; nor dare I now,
fpite of circumftances, think otherwife.

Enter LORD SPARKLE.

Spark. So, fo, Signor Quixote! What fo foon loft
your prize! Aye, you fee quarrelling for thefe virtuous
women, is as unprofitable as the affault of the windmills,
—Have you feen Lady *Bell* in my behalf?

Beauch. Lady *Bell*, my Lord! Why, fure, 'tis impoffible after your attempt on Mifs *Manners*—

Spark. Pfha! that is a ftroke in my favour. Women
like to receive the devoirs of thofe, whom others of their
fex have found fo dangerous. What did you difcover of
Lady *Bell's* fentiment towards me?

Beauch. I meant to have given the intelligence foftened,
but the agitations of my mind make it impracticable; I
muft, therefore, inform you in one word, Lady *Bell-Bloomer's*
choice is made, and that choice has not fallen upon your
Lordfhip.

Spark. Then I muft inform you in two words, that I

G 2   am

am convinced you are miſtaken. But your reaſons, Sir, your reaſons?

Beauch. Her Ladyſhip furniſhed me with a deciſive one: ſhe acknowledged a pre-engagement; and added, if I viſited her this evening, I ſhould ſee her in the preſence of the man her heart prefers.

Spark. (*laughing violently*) Excellent! charming ingenuity! Ha! ha! ha! the kindeſt, ſofteſt meſſage that ever woman fram'd; and you, like the ſheep loaden with the golden fleece, bore it, inſenſible of its value.—Ha! ha! ha! you can't ſee through the pretty artifice?

Beauch. No, really.

Spark. Why, 'tis *I* who am to be there; there by particular invitation. You'll ſee her in *my* preſence; and this was her pretty myſterious way of informing me that *I* am the object of her choice.

Beauch. Indeed!

Spark. Without a doubt! But you deep people are the dulleſt fellows at a hint; a man of half your parts would have ſeen it.—But *I* am ſatisfied, and ſhall go to her route in brilliant ſpirits.—You ſhall come, and ſee my triumph confirmed.—Come, you rogue! and ſee the lovely Widow in the preſence of the man her heart prefers.——Poor *George!* You muſt have been curſedly ſtupid, not to have conceiv'd that I was the perſon. [*Exit.* **RH**

Beauch. Yes, I will come.—Oh vanity! I had dared to explain—Yes, I conſtrued the ſweet confuſion—Oh, I bluſh at my own arrogance! Lord *Sparkle* muſt be right. —Well, this night decides it.—Narrowly will I watch each tone and look, to diſcover——Oh!—ever bleſt!—*he* whom her heart prefers! [*Exit,* **LH**

END OF THE FOURTH ACT.

29 Minutes.

Speak to Give out.

·

2 Chairs. forward.

J.W. *[signature]*

2.

ACT V. SCENE I.

An Apartment at LADY BELL'*s.* ~~A Table, with Candles~~

RH Enter LADY BELL *and* Servant.

L. Bell. ARE the tables placed in the outer room?
    Serv. Yes, Ma'am, all but the ~~Pharaoh~~ *Ecarte*
table.   *also*
  L. Bell. Then carry that there ~~too~~——I pofitively will
not have a table in the drawing-room.——[*Exit* Servant. *RH*
Thofe who play don't vifit *me*, but the card-tables; and
where they find them is very immaterial.——~~Let me fee! For~~
~~whift, Sir James Jennet——Lady Pouto~~—Mrs. *Lurchem*, and
Lady *Carmine.*——For Pharaoh, Mrs. *Evergreen*, Lord
Dangle, Sir *Harry*—Hey-dey!

LH Enter CLARINDA *and* JULIA.

  Clar. Come, child, don't faint!—You had more caufe
for terror half an hour ago.
  L. Bell. Heavens, *Julia!* where have you been? X *C.*
  Clar. Ay, that's a circumftance you would not have
known, but for an accident; and I am very forry it fell to
my lot to make the difcovery.
  L. Bell. (*taking* Julia's *hand*) Speak, my love!
  Julia. Mifs *Belmour* will tell you all fhe knows.—I am
too wretched!
  Clar. Nay, as to what I know,—I *know* very little.—I
can tell what I faw, indeed.—Having received intimations
not quite confonant to one's notions of decorum, I pretended
a frolic, and called on Mr. *Beauchamp*, and there I found
this Lady *concealed.*
  L. Bell. Heavens, *Julia!* 'Tis impoffible.
  Clar. Nay, fhe can't attempt to deny what I myfelf
faw.—Other difcoveries had liked to have been made too.

deed found there, I am not the guilty creature you imagine,
—I am married!—I will no longer conceal it! (*bursting into tears*)

L. *Bell.* Married! Oh Heavens! (*throws herself in a chair, with her back to* Julia)

Julia. I dared not reveal it to my guardian, and for that reason fled from your house.

L. *Bell.* O *Julia*, and you are married! What a serpent have I nourished!—but forgive me!—You knew not ——alas! I knew not myself, till this moment, how much——

Julia. My dearest Madam, do not add to my afflictions! —for indeed they are severe.

L. *Bell.* Ungenerous Girl! why did you conceal from me your situation?

Julia. Good Heavens! is it destin'd that one imprudent step is to lose me every blessing! In the agonies of my heart I flew to your friendship, and you kill me with reproaches.

L. *Bell.* And you have killed *me* by your want of confidence! Oh, *Julia!* had you revealed to me——

Julia. I dared not; for when Mr. *Belville* prevailed on me to give him my hand——

L. *Bell.* (*eagerly*) Mr. *Belville!*——Mr. *Belville*, say you?

Julia. Yes; it was in Paris we were married.

L. *Bell.* (*aside*) So, so, so; what a pretty mistake I made!—But it *was* a mistake! .... And so my sweet *Julia* is married! married in Paris! Sly thing! But how came you at Mr. *Beauchamp*'s, my Love?

Julia. In my rash flight this morning, my wicked Maid betray'd me into Lord *Sparkle*'s house.—There Mr. *Beauchamp* snatch'd me from ruin, and gave me a momentary asylum in his lodgings.

L. *Bell.* Did *Beauchamp!*—But what is his worth and his gallantry to me? Can't he do a right thing, but *my* heart must triumph? (*aside*)

३

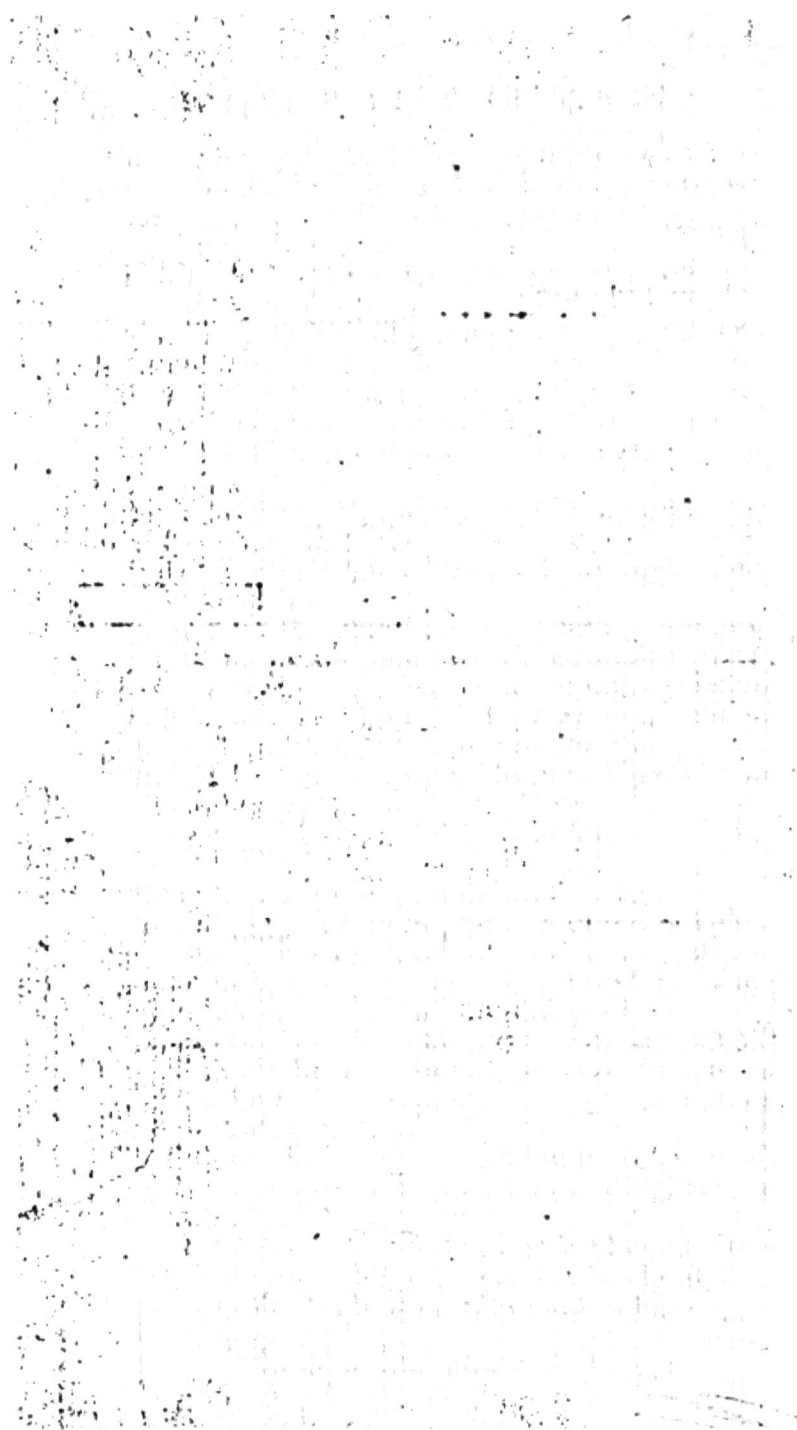

Fitz. Come, I know all; and to relieve *one* caufe
diftrefs, will tell you that the lover I fhock'd you
day, was only my agent in the little revenge I had
to take for your having married, *without* my confi
very man for whom all my cares defign'd you.

Julia. *(clafping his hands)*—Is it poffible!

Fitz. At the moment he left Paris for Florence,
ceived my directions to return home: thus *Belville*
mifs'd you, and he remain'd ignorant that you
London.

Julia. Oh Sir! had you reveal'd this to me th
ing, what evils fhould I have efcap'd?

Fitz. My dear girl, I decreed you a little puni
but your own rafhnefs has occafioned you a feverer
than you deferv'd.

L. Bell. But where is the Bridegroom? ~~I long~~
~~necromancer, whofe fpells can thaw the Veftal's b~~
~~light up flames in the cold region of a monaftery~~

Fitz. He is without, fatisfied from the mouth
champ of your conduct, *(to* Julia*)* and impatient
his *Julia* to his heart.

Julia. Oh Sir, lead me to him!—To find my
and to be forgiven by you, are felicities too great.
led by Fitzherbert.

L. Bell. What a difcovery has *Julia's* marriage
me of my own heart! I have perfuaded myfelf ~~it~~
~~paffion but the defire of conqueft~~; that it knew n
to admiration but vanity; but the pangs of jealou
to me, in one moment, that *all* its fenfe is love!

L. Bell.

An elegant Apartment lighted up, Card-parties fe
Servants carrying Refrefhments.—A Lady enters
Top of the Stage, and comes down in a hurry.

Lady. I proteft I have been three quarters of
getting from the top of the ftreet to the door!—
believe, when people give routes, they think mo
buftle they occafion without doors, than the comp
have within.

Clar. Oh yes! I am quite of that opinion.—
and racket in the ftreets are frequently the pleafa
of the entertainment; and to plague one's fobe
hours is delightful! Ha! ha! ha! My next-doc
Mrs. *Saffron,* always wheels into the country on

lic nights,—on pretence of her delicate nerves; but the truth is, her rooms will hold but fix card-tables, and mine thirteen.

1st Gent. Well, I proteft I wifh the ladies would banifh cards from their affemblies, and give us fomething in the ftyle of the *Converfaziones.*

2d Gent. Oh no, Sir *Charles*, that won't do on this fide the Alps;—we have no knack at converfation:—we think too much to be able to talk. Good talkers never think. Sir *Harry Glare*, full of bons mots, never thinks.—I myfelf am allowed to be tolerable, yet I never think.

Clar. Oh, that I believe all your friends will allow.— Hey-dey! here comes Lord *Sparkle*'s borough acquaintance —Mr. *Pendragon.*

2nd

LH Enter PENDRAGON, *meeting Clarinda & 2 Ladies RH*

Pen. Bobs, Mifs *Belmour*, how d'ye do? I didn't think to fee you.—Mr. *Fitzherbert* brought me here, and I have been examining every face, to fee if I knew any body; but fine ladies are fo alike, that one muft have long intimacy to know ones acquaintance!—Red cheeks, white necks, and fmiling lips, croud every room.

Lady. Hey-dey! a natural curiofity!—Pray, Sir, how long have you been in the world?

Pen. How long! Juft twenty years, laft Lammas.

Lady. Poh, I don't enquire into your age! How long is it fince you left your native woods?—Was you ever at a route before?

Pen. Aye, that I was, laft week!—It beat this all to nothing.—'Twas at our neighbour's the Wine-Merchant's —at his country-houfe at Kentifh-Town.

2d Lady. Oh, lud! I wifh I had been of your party! I fhould have enjoy'd a Kentifh-Town route.

Pen. Oh, you *muft* have been pleafed; for the rooms were fo little, and the company fo large, that every thing was done with one confent. We were pack'd fo clofe, that if one party moved, all the reft were obliged to obey the motion.

Lady. Delightful!—Well, Sir——

Pen. We had all the fat widows, notable miffes, and managing wives of the parifh; fo there was no fcandal, for they were *all* there.—At length the affembly broke up. —Such clattering, and *fqueedging* down the gangway ftair-cafe,

Ball Room, Screen & Back
3 & 5.16.

4.

5.

ease, whilst the little foot boy bawl'd from the passage,
" Miss *Bobbin's* bonnet is ready!"—" Mrs *Sugar-Plumb's*
" lanthorn waits!"—" Mrs. *Peppercorn's* pattens stop the
" way!" *(imitating)*

Clar. Oh, you creature, come with me! I must exhibit him in the next room. [*Exit Clarinda and* Pendragon.

Lady. Oh, stay!—Take my card.—I shall have company next Wednesday, and I insist on yours.—He is really amusing!—*(Enter Lord Sparkle from the top.)* But hide your diminish'd heads, ye Beaus and Witlings! for here comes Lord *Sparkle.* (*Exit in Centre Door to Company*)

Spark. (*speaking as he comes down*) I hope the Belles won't hide theirs; for in an age where the head is so large a part of the Lady, one should look about for the sex.

1st Gent. Well, my Lord, you see I have obey'd your summons! I shou'd not have been here, notwithstanding Lady *Bell's* invitation, had you not press'd it.

2d Gent. Nor I! I promis'd to meet a certain Lady in the Gallery at the Opera to-night,—and I regret that I did not; for I see her husband is here.—Why did you press us so earnestly to come?

Spark. Why, 'faith, to have as many witnesses as I could to my glory!—This night is given by Lady *Bell* to ME.—I am the hero of the *fete*, and expect your gratulations. Here the dear creature comes!

with L⁴ *Sparkle*

LADY BELL *comes down from the top, addressing the Company.*

L. Bell. How do you do?—how do you do? *(on each side)* You wicked creature, why did you disappoint me last night! Lady *Harriet*, I have not seen you this age! Oh, Lord *Sparkle!* I have been detain'd from my company by Mr. *Fitzherbert*, planning a scheme for *your* amusement.

Spark. Indeed! I did not expect that attention from him; tho' I acknowledge my obligations to your Ladyship's politeness.

L. Bell. *(aside)* That air of self-possession, I fancy, would be incommoded, if you guess'd at the entertainment. —Have you seen Mr. *Beauchamp?*

Spark. For a moment.—But, charming Lady *Bell*, (*taking her hand*) I shall make you expire with laughing. I really believe the poor fellow explained your message in his own favour, ha, ha, ha!

L. Bell. Ridiculous! ha, ha, ha!

H   *Enter*

Enter BEAUCHAMP. *from Top*

Beauch. Ha! 'tis true!, There they are, retired from the croud, and enjoying the privacy of lovers.

L. Bell. See there he is! I long to have a little *badinage* on the fubject.—Let us teaze him.

Spark. Oh, nothing can be more delightful!—" Hither, fighing fhepherd, come!"—Come, *Beauchamp*, take one laft, one lingering look!—fha'nt he, Lady *Bell?*

L. Bell. Doubtlefs,—if he has your Lordfhip's leave.

Spark. He feems aftonifh'd—ha, ha, ha!—Nay, it is cruel!—If the poor youth has the misfortune to be ftricken, you know he can't refift fate.—Ixion fighed for Juno.

L. Bell. Yes, and he was punifh'd too. What punifhment, Mr. *Beauchamp*, fhall we decree for you?

Beauch. I am aftonifh'd!—Was it for this your Ladyfhip commanded me to attend you?

L. Bell. How did I command you? Do you remember the words?

Beauch. I do, Madam.—You bid me come this evening, that I might behold you in the prefence of the man your heart prefers.

L. Bell. Well, Sir, and now—now you fee me!—

Spark. Oh, the fweet confufion of the fweet confeffion!
(kiffing her hand.)

Beauch. (afide) 'Sdeath! this oftentation of felicity, Madam, is ungenerous, fince you know my heart; 'tis unworthy *you!* But I *thank* you for it—I have a pang the lefs. *(going)*

L. Bell. Hold, Sir, are you going?

Beauch. This inftant, Madam.—I came in obedience to your commands; but my chaife is at your door, and before your gay affembly breaks up, I fhall be far from London, and in a day or two from England. I probably now fee your Ladyfhip for the laft time.—Adieu!

L. Bell. Stay, Mr. *Beauchamp! (agitated)*

Spark. Ay, prithee ftay! I believe Lady *Bell* has a mind to make you her conjugal father at the wedding.

Beauch. I forgive you, my Lord.—Excefs of happinefs frequently overflows into infolence, and it is the privilege of felicity to be unfeeling.—But how, Madam, has the humble paffion which has fo long confumed my life, rendered me fo hateful to *you*, as to prompt you to this barbarity? I have not *infulted* you with my love; I have
scarcely

$$\overline{\underline{6.}}$$

scarcely dared whisper it to myself: how then have I de-
served——

L. Bell. O mercy, don't be so grave! I am not insensible to your merit, nor have I beheld your passion with
disdain.—But what *can* I do? Lord *Sparkle* has so much
fashion, so much elegance—so much—

Spark. My dearest Lady *Bell*, you justify my ideas of
your discernment: and thus I thank you for the distin-
guished honour *(kneeling to kiss her hand.)*

To 2 . RH *Enter* SOPHY *from the Wing.*

Sophy. Oh you false-hearted man! *(crying)* between
Spark. *(starting up)* Hey-dey!
Sophy. Don't believe a word he says, for all you are so
fine a Lady. He'll tell you of happiness and misery, and
this, and that, and the other, but 'tis all common-place and
hyperbole—and all that sort of thing.   Because

L. Bell. Indeed! What has this young Lady claims on
your Lordship?

Spark. Claims! Ha! ha! ha! Surely your Ladyship
can answer that in a single glance. Claims! Ha! ha! ha!
Is it my fault that a little rustic does not know the language
of the day? Compliments are the ready coin of conversation, and 'tis every one's business to understand their
value.

RH Enter PENDRAGON. To 2 .

Pen. *(clapping him on the shoulder)* True, my Lord,
true;—and pray instruct me what was the value of the
compliment, when you told me I should make a figure in
the Guards, and that you would speak to your great friends
to make me a colonel?

Spark. Value! Why, of just as much as it would bring!
You thought it so valuable then, that you got me a hundred extra votes on the strength of it; and you are now
a little ungrateful wretch, to pretend 'twas worth nothing.

LH Enter FITZHERBERT, *leading* JULIA.

Fitz. But here, Lord *Sparkle*, is a Lady who claims a
right on a different foundation. She had no Election inte-
rest to provoke your flatteries, yet you have not scrupled to
profess love to her, whilst under the roof of her friend,
whose hand you was soliciting in marriage.

Julia. Yes, I intreat your Ladyſhip not to fancy that you are to break the hearts of half our ſex by binding Lord *Sparkle* in the adamantine chains of marriage.—I boaſt an equal right with you, and don't flatter yourſelf I ſhall reſign him.

Spark. Mere malice, Lady *Bell!* *Fitzberbert's* malice! ——I never had a ſerious thought of Miſs *Manners* in my life.

LH Enter BELVILLE.

Bel. What, my Lord! and have you dared talk of love to that Lady without a ſerious thought?

Spark. Hey dey! what right have you——

Bel. Oh, very trifling! only the right of a Huſband—The Lady ſo honour'd by your love-making *in jeſt* is my wife; in courſe, all obligations to her devolve on me.

Spark. Your wife! My dear *Belville,* I give you joy with all my ſoul! You ſee 'tis always dangerous to keep ſecrets from your friends. But is any body elſe coming? Have I any new crimes to be accus'd of? Any more witneſſes coming to the bar?

Bel. No; but I am a witneſs in a new cauſe, and accuſe you of loading the mind of my friend *Beauchamp* with a ſenſe of obligation you had neither ſpirit or juſtice to confer.

Lady Bell. A Commiſſion, my Lord, which was ſent Mr. *Beauchamp* under a blank cover, by one who could not bear to ſee his noble ſpirit dependent on your caprices.

Belv. And when his ſentiments pointed out your Lordſhip as his benefactor, you accepted the honour, and have laid heavy taxes on his gratitude.

Spark. Well, and what is there in all that? *Beauchamp* did not know to whom he was obliged; and wou'dn't it have been a moſt unchriſtian thing to let a good action run about the world belonging to nobody?—I found it a ſtray orphan, and ſo father'd it.——But you, *Fitzherbert,* I ſee are the lawful owner of the brat; ſo prithee take it back, and thank me for the honour of my patronage.

Fitz. Your affected pleaſantry, Lord *Sparkle,* may ſhield you from reſentment, but it will not from contempt. Your effrontery——

Spark. Effrontery! Prithee make diſtinctions!—What in certain lines would be effrontery, in me is only the eaſe of Faſhion; that delightful thing, which enables me at this moment to ſtand ſerene amidſt your meditated ſtorm.——

Come,

Come, my dear Lady *Bell*, let us leave thefe good gentry, and love ourfelves amidft the delights of fafhion, and the charms of *bon ton*.

Lady Bell. Pardon me, my Lord! As caprice is abfolutely neceffary to the character of a fine lady, you will not be furpris'd if I give an inftance of it now; and, fpite of your elegance, your fafhion, and your wit, prefent my hand to this poor foldier—who boafts only worth, fpirit, honour, and love.

Beauch. Have a care, Madam!—Feelings like mine are not to be trifled with! Once already the hopes you have infpir'd——

Lady Bell. The hour of *trifling* is paft; and furely it cannot appear extraordinary, that I prefer the internal worth of an uncorrup'ed heart, to the outward polifh of a mind too feeble to fupport itfelf againft vice, in the feductive forms of fafhionable diffipation.

Spark. Hey-dey! what, is your Ladyfhip in the plot?

Fitz. The plot has been deeper laid than you, my Lord, have been able to conceive. As I have the misfortune to be related to you, I thought it my duty to watch over your conduct. I have feen your plans, which generally tended to your confufion and difgrace; and many of them have been defeated, tho' you knew not by what means. But what fate does your Lordfhip defign for thefe young people, decoy'd by you from their native ignorance and home?

Spark. Let them return to their native ignorance and home as faft as they can.

Pend. No, no; hang me if I do that!—I know Life now, and Life I'll have—Hyde-Park, Plays, Operas, and all that fort of thing.—But, Old Gentleman, as you promis'd to do fomething for me, what think ye of a Commiffion?—The Captain there can't want his now; fuppofe you turn it over to me?

Fitz. No, young man, you fhall be taken care of; but the requifites of a foldier are not thofe of pertnefs and affurance. Intrepid fpirit, nice honour, generofity, and underftanding, all unite to form him.—It is thefe which will make a Britifh foldier once again the firft character in Europe.—It is fuch foldiers who muft make England once again invincible, and her glittering arms triumphant in every quarter of the globe.

Sophy. Well, *Bobby* may do as he will—I'll go back to Cornwall directly, and warn all my neighbours to take

fpecial

special care how they trust to a Lord's promises at an Election again. (*and Exit R*)

Spark. Well, great attempts and great failings mark the life of a man of spirit!—There is eclat even in my disappointment to-night; and I am ready for a fresh set of adventures to-morrow.

Fitz. Incorrigible man!—But I have done with *you.*— *Beauchamp* has answered all my hopes, and the discernment of this charming woman, in rewarding him, merits the happiness that awaits her; and that I may give the fullest sanction to her choice, I declare *him* heir to my estate. This, I know, is a stroke your Lordship did not expect.

Beauch. And was it then to you, Sir!—The tumults of my gratitude——

Fitz. Your conduct has completely rewarded me; and in adopting you——

Lady Bell. (*interrupting*) Oh, I protest against that!— Our union would then appear a prudent, *sober* business, and I should lose the credit of having done a mad thing for the sake of the man—my heart prefers.

Fitz To you I resign him with pleasure: his fate is in your hands.

Lady Bell. Then he shall continue a soldier—one of those whom Love and his Country detain to guard her dearest, *last* possessions.

Beauch. Love and my Country! Yes, ye shall divide my heart.——Animated by such passions, our forefathers were invincible; and if we wou'd preserve the freedom and independence they obtain'd for us, we must imitate their virtues.

F I N I S.

www.ingramcontent.com/pod-product-compliance
Lightning Source LLC
Chambersburg PA
CBHW030547270326
41927CB00008B/1552